MEN ARE FROM
LOCKER ROOMS
WOMEN ARE FROM
LUXURY BOXES

A Woman's "Survival" Guide to Understanding Spectator Sports

Laurie Selwitz

ZuMedia
Los Angeles, California

Men Are From Locker Rooms, Women Are From Luxury Boxes

Copyright © 1998 by Laurie Selwitz
All rights reserved

Published by: ZuMedia
P.O. Box 252352
Los Angeles, CA 90025

Printed in the United States of America
First Printing: February 1999

Library of Congress Cataloging-in-Publication Data
Selwitz, Laurie

Men Are From Locker Rooms, Women Are From Luxury Boxes: A Woman's "Survival" Guide to Understanding Spectator Sports/Laurie Selwitz - 1st ed.

ISBN 0-9667627-9-7

Illustrations by Jonathan Kennedy
Cover Art by Jon Murphy - Beynon Company, Los Angeles
Title by Michael E. Anzis

ACKNOWLEDGEMENTS

♥ ♥

There are so many people I need to thank for all the help and support they've given me over the last few months. I guess I should start by thanking my father for molding me into the son he never had. Thank you, dad – for everything. I couldn't have done it without you. And to Mom and Aaron, Julie, Mike and Carol – thank you for believing in me every step of the way. I am so fortunate to have such a supportive and loving family.

I am also very fortunate to have had some wonderful people so generously donate their time, share their expertise, and offer their advice:

To Karen Newman - hockey connoisseur and goaltender extraordinaire – thank you for all your help, and for your support and sense of humor from day one.

To Roy Hamilton - one of my first memories of UCLA basketball (I wasn't that young!), thank you for your constant thoughtfulness and generosity.

To Steve Physioc - I really enjoyed our "Angels" talks. Thanks for indulging me, and for all your help throughout the season.

To Brian Baldinger and Scott Tinsley - thank you both for helping me to better understand and communicate a very difficult and technical sport.

To Suszi Lurie and Peter Freyer – not many people would pick up a pen and start writing if I dropped this in their laps and said "make this better", but you guys did. Thank you!

And last, but not least, to my friend, and illustrator, Jon Kennedy - you never cease to amaze me with your talents. Thank you from the bottom of my heart – I couldn't have asked for more!

♥ ♥

TABLE OF CONTENTS

PREFACE

A couple of years ago I invited a girlfriend of mine to a hockey game. It took a bit of persuasion on my part due to the fact that never having been to a game, she could only imagine what she was in for – a little skating, a lot of blood, and a wasted evening. That, I assured her, would not be the case. She agreed to go. Well, a couple of beers and hot dogs later, I was amazed to find her completely caught up in the energy and excitement, and actually enjoying the game. And I remember thinking what a shame it was that more women weren't into hockey because we were having such a great time. (Although I'm not saying it's a bad thing that there are tons of men at hockey games!)

So there we were, yelling and screaming, clapping and cheering, when she turned to me and said "Let's walk around at half-time, okay?" Needless to say, throughout the evening I had explained to her many of the finer points of the game, including that in hockey, there is no half-time. And by the end of the game, she was already making plans to go to another one. I wasn't surprised. She later admitted to me that the reason she'd been so reluctant to go to a game, any game, with me was that she didn't understand them. Now that she did, she was hooked.

Imagine going to see a foreign film – you don't understand the language and there are no subtitles. Not easy to sit through, is it? It's the same thing with sports – the more you understand, the more enjoyable the experience. Learning the rules of the game should be as enjoyable as the game itself.

And that is why I wrote this book. Most of the books out there for the amateur fan are either written on an elementary level, or are too advanced, too technical, and take for granted most of the basics you need to know. In a nutshell – they're boring. This book, I guarantee you, will be a fun read. But most importantly, it will teach you everything you need to know to make watching a game fun. Because if it's not fun, what's the point?!

INTRODUCTION

It's a beautiful day. The sun is shining, the birds are singing, and you can't wait to go out and enjoy those warm skies and fresh air. You optimistically tell the man in your life about your plans for the day, and he says, "Sorry, hon, but I can't go out, it's..."

Sunday - Football. All day.

Monday - Football. And of course he has to watch Monday Night Live following the game because he's got to see all the highlights and analysis.

Tuesday - You remember, he plays basketball with the guys on Tuesday nights.

Wednesday - National Hockey Night on ESPN. It's been awhile since he's seen a good fight.

Thursday - The Lakers are in town. And he's gotta see what color that crazy guy Dennis Rodman's hair is this week.

Friday - He's exhausted and wants to order in Chinese and call it an early night. After all, tomorrow is...

Saturday - College hoops. Again, all day. And he's got to keep up on all the teams if he wants to enter the NCAA tournament office pool.

Sound familiar? Well, as one wise person once said, "If you can't beat 'em, join 'em." Now hold on, before you say no, decide it's the day you need to clip your dog's toenails, or remember you have to drive your Aunt Sally to the airport across town, consider the **top 10 benefits** that can come from watching sports:

10. Save big bucks by watching the game and cooking at home rather than spending a fortune on dinner and a movie. (And you get to stay in your comfy sweats and t-shirt!)

9. The camaraderie of the Monday morning big games review at the water cooler.

8. Convince him to spend Sunday mornings snuggling in bed with you.

7. The ability to talk to any guy – any time, any place.

6. Release stress and built-up tension from cheering and shouting. (And no, the players and referees on TV can't hear you, guys just think they can).

5. The pleasure that comes from yelling, "hey, hon, get me another beer, would ya?"

4. Make him happy by taking an interest in something that he enjoys.

3. All those gorgeous hunks in tight uniforms.

2. Spend more quality time with your guy.

...and the number 1 benefit that comes from watching sports...

1. The discovery that you, too, can have fun and end up loving sports.

Okay, the ball is now in your court. I know all this new information may feel a bit overwhelming, so do what the guys do before a big game – grab a snack and cold drink, put your feet up, get comfortable, and enjoy!

BASEBALL

Baseball. America's favorite pastime. And do you want to know why? Because after all this time, it is still the most affordable sport around. It's almost cheaper to get a massage, a haircut, *and* a manicure than it is to go to a hockey or football game. At a baseball game, ten bucks will buy you a ticket, a hot dog, <u>and</u> a beer. What a bargain! And the ballpark is a great place to spend a sunny summer afternoon.

<u>THE GAME</u>

Baseball differs from the other three sports (basketball, football, & hockey) in that it is the only sport that is not run by a clock. There is no time limit, and the length of the game (playing time) is never the same. (As in contrast with, say, hockey, which is always 60 minutes, or 65 with an overtime period.) Baseball is played in **innings**, the period of play in which each team has a turn at bat. Each inning is divided into the **top of the inning**, when the first team is at bat, and the **bottom of the inning**, when the second team is at bat. So what would you call the period between the top and bottom of the inning? No, not a bathroom break, although that's a pretty good guess. And okay, so maybe it is a good time to get another beer. But I was kind-of going for middle of the inning. As the length of each game differs, so does the length of each inning. A typical game usually lasts around 3 hours. There are nine innings in a game, and if at the end of nine innings the game is tied, **extra innings** are played until one team scores the winning run(s). But extra innings are just like the first nine – if one team scores in the top of the inning, the other team still gets the opportunity to bat in the bottom of the inning.

THE PLAYING FIELD

The **field**, commonly referred to as the **diamond**, is made of either grass or AstroTurf (fake grass). Sure doesn't sound like a girl's best friend to me! It is divided into the infield and the outfield, and unlike in other sports, in baseball there aren't "side lines" or "end lines" which so easily define the "inbounds" area. Instead, two foul lines determine whether the ball has been hit in fair or foul territory.

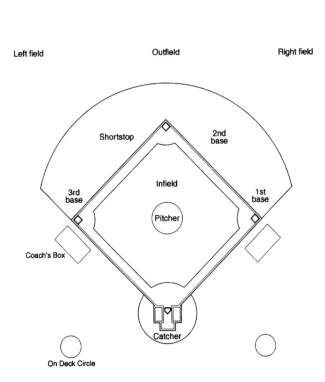

14

The Infield

The **infield** is basically a big square area with a base in each corner, a pitcher's mound in the middle, and several chalk field-markings. The bases, **1st base**, **2nd base**, **3rd base**, and the 4th base, known as **home plate**, are 90 feet apart from each other. You may occasionally hear a base referred to as a **bag**. The path(s) that connect the four bases are called the **base lines**.

Speaking of bases... before we get into the game itself, I think it's important that you understand why baseball is such a big part of a guy's life. It actually starts very early. You see, as the adolescent male becomes interested in the opposite sex, he zeros in on one sweet, innocent, unsuspecting young girl. They go to a movie, or out for a soda, and what is the first thing his buddies ask him the next day? Exactly - did he get to first base. As the boy gets older - you know, 15 or 16 - what is at the back of his mind 24 hours a day? *If you don't get to first base, you're never going to score.* And that is why, from childhood, baseball is subconsciously rooted deep into the souls of all boys. Okay, back to the game.

The **pitcher's mound** is in the middle of the infield, and is raised 10 inches above field level. The pitcher stands on a plate, known as the **pitching rubber**. Now here's a little insider's lingo for you. The pitcher's mound is often referred to as "the hill". Example - instead of saying, "Jim Smith is pitching for the Giants", you could say "Jim Smith is *on the hill* for the Giants". So, is "on the hill" another term for pitcher? I don't think so. But go ahead, throw that one around at the office and see if a few heads don't turn!

Home plate is surrounded by several chalk markings. On each side of home plate is a **batter's box** - one for left handed batters & one for right handed batters - where the batters stand as they attempt to hit the ball. Now, there are some players who "swing both ways", and are known as **switch hitters**. Oh, get your mind out of the gutter - it has nothing to do with their sexual preferences. It just means they can bat both left and right handed. Behind home plate is the **catcher's box**, and the catcher must stay in it while waiting for a pitch.

The Outfield

The **outfield**, which extends outwards from the perimeter of the baselines to a wall or fence, is divided into 3 sections; **left field, center field**, and **right field**. But unlike the standard football field, hockey rink, and basketball court, the size of a baseball field differs from ballpark to ballpark. (Which is okay, because not everybody thinks size is <u>that</u> important!) Some of the variables are the distances from home plate to the left field wall, center field wall, and right field wall.

Foul Territory

Two **foul lines**, meeting at home plate and forming a 90 degree angle, divide fair from foul territory. If the ball crosses over the foul line <u>before</u> it reaches 1st/3rd base, it is considered foul. But if it crosses the foul line <u>after</u> it passes 1st/3rd base, it is a fair ball. The outside of 1st and 3rd base coincide with the foul lines, which extend to the end of the outfield marked by a **foul pole**. If the ball rolls over a base, it is considered a fair ball. If the ball hits the foul pole, it is a home run. (I know, it should be called a "fair" pole!)

bullpen

The players' benches are in the **dugouts**, which are below ground level, along the 1st and 3rd base lines in foul territory. The team on offense waits in the dugout, <u>except</u> for the player due up next to bat, referred to as the player **on deck**. He waits in the **on-deck circle**, which is between the dugout and home plate. The **bullpen** is the area in foul territory where relief pitchers practice, and wait to be called into the game. Who comes up with these terms? On deck - where is he, on a ship or something? And the bullpen - sounds like a bunch of cattle rounded-up and fenced in, biding their time until they become a vegetarian's worst nightmare.

EQUIPMENT

Baseball players don't wear much in the way of protective clothing, with the exception of the catcher. The catcher wears a lot of protective gear including a metal mask, a chest/stomach protector, shin guards, and a helmet. Ever played target practice - and been the target? It's one thing to have those fast balls coming at you while standing up. But I don't think those catchers, who stay squatted down real low, have quite the same ability to always react quickly and dodge those bullets.

The fielders use **gloves**, although the 1st basemen and catchers' gloves are referred to as **mitts**. They also wear shoes with spikes on the bottom, known as **cleats**, for better traction when a field is wet and slippery. When a player is at bat, he must wear a **batting helmet**, to protect his head in case he gets nailed with a fast ball. But I'm pretty sure that a player hit with a ball going 90 miles an hour will still be seeing double for awhile, helmet or no helmet.

The **baseball**, which basically is small enough to be gripped with one hand, can reach speeds of up to 100 miles per hour, and distances of more than 400 feet. In professional baseball, players can only use a **bat** made of wood - no aluminium. I'm not quite sure why, some say it's due to the increased speed of the ball hit off an aluminium bat, and this is an attempt at reducing injuries. Some say it could be due to the treacherous weather these guys are sometimes forced to play in - aluminium bats… rain… thunder… lightning... You do the math!

THE PLAYERS

A baseball team is made up of 25 players, with 9 players in the game at a time. Every player has both an offensive and defensive role to play. When a team is on offense, they are **at bat**. When they are on defense, they are **on the field**. So who determines which team bats first? That is easily and quickly resolved - the visiting team always bats first, in the **top of the inning**. Therefore, the home team takes the field.

Offense

The object of the game is to score more runs than the other team. A **run** is equivalent to a point. Each time an offensive player safely reaches home plate, he is credited with one run. How does a player reach home plate? Well, he must advance around the four bases, in order, without being tagged or thrown out. (Luckily, in baseball, a guy can't lie and tell his buddies he scored when in actuality he never even made it to second base!) A **home run** is when a player hits the ball over the outfield wall in fair territory. This allows all base runners, including the batter, to score a run.

So, we know that the visiting team starts the game at bat, but which player bats first? The best hitter? The worst? The tallest? And who bats second? Do they flip a coin? Fortunately, that is something the players don't have to worry about. Before each game, the manager puts together a **batting order**, also known as the **line-up**. He takes many things into consideration, for example, a batter's hitting style and skill, how they match up against the opposing pitcher, and who is on a hot streak.

The first batter, known as the **lead-off hitter**, must be good and consistent at getting on base. (For all the money these guys are making, shouldn't they all be good and consistent at getting on base?!)

The second batter should be skilled at advancing the runner on base. (The most common way is bunting, which I'll cover a little later.)

The third batter is usually the best hitter, with the best **batting average** - the number of hits divided by the number of times at bat.

The fourth batter, also known as the **clean-up hitter**, is a "power" hitter, expected to "clean" the bases of the runners, allowing them to score. And hopefully, in this situation, you won't hear a bunch of guys whining *"I'm not cleaning up."* *"Well, I'm not cleaning up, it's not my mess"*...

The fifth and sixth batters, also power hitters, are expected to drive in the runs the 4th batter didn't.

The seventh and eighth batters are - how can I say this nicely - not exactly the best hitters on the team. Didn't your mother always tell you, *if you can't say something nice, don't say anything at all?* Okay, easy enough, the 7th and 8th batters excel at their defensive roles.

Now, the ninth batter could be either of two players. In the National League, the 9th batter is usually the pitcher. But in the American League, the pitcher does not bat. Instead, a **designated hitter**, commonly referred to as the **DH**, takes the pitcher's place at bat, but does not play a defensive position on the field. Designated hitter... he only hits... okay, you get it. Actually, you will often see the designated hitter placed somewhere in the middle of the line-up, another variable that can change from game to game. (The National and American Leagues will be covered in more detail at the end of the chapter.)

There are basically four different ways the ball can be hit:

- A **ground ball** is when the ball rolls or bounces on the ground before the fielder **gloves** (picks up) the ball.
- A **fly ball** is hit high in the air.
- A **line drive** is a hard hit ball that travels a few feet above the ground.
- A **bunt** is when a player just taps the ball a few feet from home plate, sacrificing himself as he is thrown out at first base, in an attempt to advance the runner(s). Sometimes if the bunt surprises the infield, the batter can make it safely to first base.

When a batter either hits the ball, or walks, and it allows a teammate to advance to home plate, the batter is credited with a **run batted in**, also referred to as an **RBI**.

Every sport has substitutes, and baseball is no different. Most substitutes in baseball are either hitters, known as **pinch hitters**, or pitchers, known as **relief pitchers**. Pinch hitters usually come in when a team is behind (losing) to replace a "weaker" hitter. Now, I bet you probably think that would be the 7th or 8th batter, but that's not necessarily always the case. Everyone has "off" games, even the best players. And, sometimes, the batters with the lowest batting averages are "on", and have an outstanding game offensively. A substitute can come into the game at any time, for either team, but once a player leaves the game he cannot return.

Defense

As the home team takes the field, each player stations himself at a designated position. The **infielders** are the **1st baseman**, **2nd baseman**, **3rd baseman**, and the **shortstop**, who is positioned between the 2nd and 3rd basemen. The **pitcher** is on the pitcher's mound, and the **catcher** is behind home plate in the catcher's box. The **outfielders** are the **left fielder**, **center fielder**, and **right fielder**. Pretty simple stuff so far, huh? All right then - let me increase the level of difficulty just a bit. Each defensive position is numbered.

The reason why is when the announcers are calling a play, using position numbers makes it a lot easier and quicker. The positions are numbered as follows:

1. Pitcher (P)
2. Catcher (C)
3. 1st Baseman (1B)
4. 2nd Baseman (2B)
5. 3rd Baseman (3B)

6. Short Stop (SS)
7. Left Fielder (LF)
8. Center Fielder (CF)
9. Right Fielder (RF)

Let's say the batter hits the ball to the short stop, who in turn throws the ball to the 1st baseman for the out. Instead of saying the runner was thrown out at 1st base by the shortstop, it's a lot easier to say the runner was out 6 - 3. It's not critical to know this, it just makes it a little easier to follow the game when listening to the announcers. Think of it as extra credit.

The objective of the defensive team is to **retire**, meaning put out, three (offensive) players before they score any runs. When I say "retire", I'm not talking about how a player plans his retirement, you know, by demanding an astronomically high salary for a few years so that he may enjoy a care-free life of luxury, obtaining every monetary pleasure desired.

retiring a batter

Don't worry, his friends - Mr. Basketball Player, Mr. Football Player, and Mr. Hockey Player - are not to be left out. They are all rewarded, and retire, with exactly the same benefits, if not more.

When 3 offensive players have been put out, it is also referred to as **retiring the side** (team). There are basically three ways to retire a batter:

- Strike him out.
- If the ball is hit, catch it before it touches the ground. (A line drive or fly ball.)
- Tag, or force, him out with the ball while he is running between the bases.

Now, sometimes in an attempt to throw out the batter, or another base runner, the fielder will make a mistake which allows the runner to safely reach the base. This would be known as an **error**. For example, say the batter hits the ball to the short stop but the ball bounces off his glove. If he can't quite get a hold of the ball right away, he might rush the throw to 1st base, sending the ball over the head of the 1st baseman. The batter would not only be safe at 1st base, but depending on where the ball ended up, he could possibly even make it to 2nd base. In this case, the batter would not be credited with a hit. Instead, the short stop would be charged with the error. Well, let's get back to retiring a batter. The first way, striking him out, is accomplished by the pitcher. So, let's talk a little bit about the pitcher.

The Pitcher

As it is the defense's objective to keep the offense from scoring, it is the pitcher's objective to keep the bases empty. You know, I could be talking about pitchers, and even be so specific as to put it under the heading of "different players on the field", and many guys would still probably think, *Hey, pitchers. Cool. Fill mine up with Budweiser.* One track minds. Well, two, but notice I said different players, not positions, on the field. You've heard the saying, *for every action there is a reaction*? Well, that pretty much describes the game of baseball, and it all starts with the pitcher. He throws the ball, the batter reacts to the pitch, and consequently, the players on the field react to the batter.

Play begins with the pitcher throwing the ball to the batter. Throwing the ball can't be that tough, can it? Well, throwing it is one thing, but getting it in the strike zone is another. The **strike zone** is different with each batter, but it is basically the area over home plate, which is 17 inches wide, and between the batter's shoulders and knees. And don't think the batter won't "crouch" down as much as he can to make the strike zone as small as possible. If the ball just barely goes over one corner of the plate, it is still considered in the strike zone. You might hear an umpire call a pitch **high and inside**, meaning, the ball was thrown above the shoulders (high), and in between the plate and the batter (inside). Because the strike zone is different with every player, some pitches are difficult to call. Although, sometimes some of the calls are so bad that you'll wonder whether or not it's the umpire who's high. The batter can swing at any pitch, in or out of the strike zone, if he thinks he can hit it.

Each player is given three strikes and four balls to get on base. The number of balls and strikes a batter has is known as the **count**, with the number of balls indicated first. For example, a count of 2 and 1 would be two balls and one strike. A count of 3 and 2 is known as a **full count**. Why? Because the next pitch, a 4th ball or 3rd strike and that player's turn at bat is over. A **ball** is called when a pitch is thrown outside of the strike zone and the batter does not swing at it. A **strike** is called when:

- The batter swings at a pitch, regardless of whether it's in or out of the strike zone, but misses the ball.
- The batter **takes a strike**, which means he does not swing at a pitch that is thrown in the strike zone.

- The batter hits the ball into foul territory - <u>unless</u> the batter already has two strikes.

A batter who has two strikes against him can keep hitting the ball into foul territory, as many times as necessary, until he either; **1.**) hits the ball into fair territory, **2.**) strikes out by swinging and missing the ball, **3.**) "takes" the 3rd called strike, or **4.**) gets a 4th ball called. Remember, one of the ways to retire a batter is by catching a fly ball. And it's no different if that fly ball is hit foul - if it's caught, the batter is out. A variation of this would be the **foul tip** (a concept most waitresses are unfortunately quite familiar with.) If the batter hits the ball straight back and it is caught by the catcher, the batter is out, even if it's his first strike. If it is not caught, it is exactly the same as hitting the ball foul.

strike

When the batter has three strikes called, he has struck out and his turn at bat is over. <u>But</u> - there is one exception to this rule, known as the **wild pitch rule**. That is a pitch that gets away from the catcher and allows the runner(s) to advance. If a batter strikes out, and 1st base is empty - and only when 1st base is empty - the batter can advance to first base. But the catcher, if he's quick, still has the opportunity to throw him out at first.

If the pitcher throws four balls before the batter either hits the ball or receives three strikes, the batter takes a **base on balls**, also referred to as a **walk**. It really should be called a jog, rather than a walk, as I have never seen a batter walk over to first base. He doesn't walk, he doesn't run - he jogs. Anyway, he automatically advances to first base. And the player(s) on the base(s) <u>directly</u> in front of him - with no empty bases between them - also walk(s). For example, if there is a runner on 1st base, he advances to 2nd. A runner on 2nd would only advance if there is a runner at 1st. There is one other situation when the batter automatically walks, no matter what the count is, and that is when he is hit by a pitch. Fortunately it doesn't happen too often.

Sometimes a pitcher will intentionally walk a batter, called an **intentional walk**, for one of two reasons; 1.) there is a runner on 2nd base, and the pitcher wants to get the batter to 1st base, increasing the chances of a double play, or 2.) the pitcher wants to avoid a particular batter, especially if a weaker batter follows. Just think how good that makes the player who follows the intentional walk feel. *Your friend there is pretty tough, so I think I'll intentionally walk him. But you, hey, no problem.*

Now, in what situation would a pitcher never intentionally walk a batter? Right - when the **bases are loaded**, which means, there are runners on every base; 1st, 2nd, and 3rd. Remember - when a batter is walked, all runners directly in front of one another get to advance one base. That means the runner on 3rd would walk in to score a run. And that's not good. It actually kind-of makes the pitcher look bad. Ouch!

So you can see the pitcher has a very tough job. And it's not only because the game can often be won or lost by his performance, but also because he also has many rules he must follow:

- The pitcher's back foot must remain on the pitching rubber until he lets go of the ball. This rule ensures that he stays the legal distance from home plate.

- A pitcher cannot catch a batter off guard by delivering a quick pitch. The batter must be in position and ready to hit, or the pitch doesn't count.

- The pitcher must step toward 1st base if he is going to throw there. He can't pretend to be throwing to home plate, then turn and throw to 1st base. Which also means he can't try and fool the batter by stepping toward 1st base and then throwing a pitch. (No games of "Psych!" with the base runner!) We'll talk about throwing out a base runner a little later.

- The pitcher has twenty seconds to throw the ball after getting it back from the catcher/umpire.

- The pitcher can't apply anything to the ball, i.e. spit, sweat, Vaseline, or whatever other attractive enhancements he can think of. That is why the umpire keeps a "fresh" ball in play at all times. Speaking of spitting... baseball players are always spitting and scratching themselves... such attractive qualities in a man, don't you think?

- Once the wind-up motion has begun, the pitcher must follow it through and complete the pitch to home plate. Failure to do so results in the umpire calling a **balk** - failure by the pitcher to complete his delivery (after the wind-up) with one or more runners on base. Basically, he can't start his wind-up and then stop. If he does, the runners all get to advance one base. If there are no runners on base, a ball is called.

So, when there is a runner on base, the pitcher doesn't do a full wind-up. Why? Because it gives the runner a chance to **steal** - when the runner takes off early, usually while the pitcher is winding up, and makes it to the next base before the catcher can throw him out. So instead of a wind-up, he uses more of a stretching motion. He lifts both hands to about head level, lowers them down to his chest, and then has the choice to either pitch the ball to the batter **or** throw the ball to the base. But remember, he must step toward 1st base if he's going to throw there.

Now while the catcher is trying to throw out runners before they get to the next base, the pitcher will also try to catch a runner just a couple of steps too many off the base and throw him out before he can get back safely. This is known as a **pick-off**. In a pick-off, the baseman must tag the runner, not just have his foot on the base. Occasionally you may see the pitcher intentionally throw the ball outside the strike zone so the catcher has a better chance to throw out a base runner trying to steal. This is known as a **pitch-out**.

stealing a base

Types of Pitches

Have you ever watched a game, at the stadium or on TV, and heard the announcer call the different types of pitches on delivery - fastball, knuckleball, curveball... - and wondered how in the heck he could tell the difference between any of them when they're flying by at 90 miles an hour? They all sure look like fastballs to me. Obviously they're seasoned professionals and it's second nature to them, but for most of us, they're incredibly difficult, if not impossible, to distinguish. Well, just in case you're just a little bit curious, and would like to know just what these elusive pitches entail, read on.

There are basically four pitches, and although there are several variations to each one, I'm going to try to keep this very basic. The four pitches, starring in alphabetical order, are the curveball, fastball, knuckleball, and slider.

The **curveball** is delivered straight to the plate, but hooks (curves) away from, or into, the batter as it reaches the plate. (With a right handed pitcher, it'll curve away from a right handed batter, and curve into a left handed batter, and visa versa.) The pitcher does this by releasing the ball with a twist or snap of the wrist. When the ball hooks in, instead of out, it is known as a **screwball**. So, basically, it's a pitch that appears to be going one way, then quickly changes directions. Very similar to when a guy throws a girl a curveball. One minute he loves her, and then - wham! - he needs his space. And often, neither the batter nor the girl saw it coming.

The **fastball** is thrown at full speed. Gee, what a surprise that is. And it gets to the plate in less than one second. So I guess the curveball is considered slow because it only goes 85 instead of 95 miles an hour? I think I'll stick to softball - now that's an under-handed "slow" pitch (toss) I can handle!

The **knuckleball** travels very slowly, 60 to 65 miles per hour, and breaks as it nears the batter. The pitcher grips the ball with his knuckles (or fingertips) and thumb, and doesn't snap his wrist, which results in no spin on the delivery. But it gives the illusion of the ball jumping around all the way to the plate, which makes it really tough to hit. (It's also very difficult to catch.)

The **slider** is somewhat a cross between the fastball and the curveball. It is a fastball with a slight (unpredictable) break as it approaches the batter. It is thrown like a fastball, but the pitcher turns his wrist as he releases the ball. This pitch is about 5 – 7 miles an hour slower than the fastball.

Often you will hear the announcers referring to the pitch as a **change-up**. What that means is a pitcher will change the speed of the pitch to confuse the batter. For example, a pitcher might throw two fastballs in a row, and when the batter expects another fastball, he throws a slowball, intended to mess up a batter's timing as the change-up can be up to 15 miles an hour slower than the fastball.

Now, as I said, there are many variations to these pitches, for example, the split-finger fastball, or the forkball. But do you really want to get that technical? I didn't think so.

Relief Pitchers

No, they're not back-up pitchers of beer for when the first one is emptied. They're the guys who come into the game to take over for the starting pitcher. A starting pitcher rarely pitches a full game. There are too many games in the season, and they need to rest their (pitching) arms as much as possible. Good pitching arms are a rare, and very valuable, commodity. So, when a team wins, which pitcher is credited with the win?

For a **starting pitcher** to get credit for the **win**, he must pitch at least 5 2/3 complete innings, and have the lead when he goes out. If after he leaves the game the team loses the lead, he is credited with what is referred to as a **no-decision**, which is neither a win or a loss on his record.

- When the starting pitcher pitches all 9 innings, he has pitched a **complete game**.

- If the starting pitcher hasn't given up any runs, he has pitched a **shut-out**.

- If the starting pitcher retires all 27 batters in a row (allowed no hits <u>or</u> walks), he has pitched a **perfect game**.

If the **relief pitcher** comes in <u>before</u> the fifth inning and maintains the lead, he will be credited with the **win**. Or, if he comes in when the team is tied or behind, and the team goes ahead while he is in, he would also get the win. Those would be in cases when the starting pitcher is, basically, choking. Or, you could just say he's having an off day - don't we all?! A team may use more than one relief pitcher in one game. In that case, the official scorer decides which pitcher was most effective, and credits him with the win. That is, of course, if after bringing in multiple relief pitchers, they are able to pull off the win.

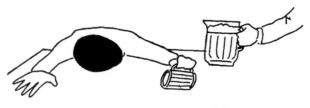

relief pitcher

Let's face it - if a team is winning, it is usually with effective pitching, and bringing in numerous relief pitchers should not be necessary. You know the old saying, *if it ain't broke, don't fix it.*

When a team is ahead by just a couple runs, they will often bring in a special relief pitcher, known as the **closer**, to secure the win. If the team is ahead by three or less runs, and the closer gets the win, he is credited with what is known as a **save**. The save is <u>very</u> important, for it is his job, and specialty, to end the game and get that win. Nobody likes to see a lead blown in the 9th inning, but if that happens, the closer is credited with what is affectionately known as a **blown save**.

<u>The Catcher</u>

The catcher's job is more important than it may appear. He's not just playing catch with the pitcher. He is the one who actually determines which pitch (fastball, curveball...) the pitcher should throw. They use a sort-of secret code/sign language to communicate - they don't want to give anything away to the batter! Sometimes the pitcher won't like the call and he'll signal to the catcher to change it. But what's important is that these two guys have good chemistry (no, not the same kind of chemistry we'd all like to have with Mr. Right!) and are on the same wavelength. That's why you will often see certain catchers playing on days that specific pitchers play. Another important responsibility of the catcher is to throw out runners attempting to steal a base. So he really needs to stay alert, be quick, and have a very accurate arm.

BASE RUNNING

This probably sounds like the easiest part of any player's game, but, actually, this is what separates the men from the boys. Okay, maybe I'm being a tad dramatic, but good base running takes skill, experience, and smarts. Let's go back to retiring the batter. The first way was to strike him out. The second way is to catch the line drive or fly ball before it touches the ground, which is pretty self-explanatory. The third way is to tag, or force, a player out with the ball.

What's the difference between a force and a tag? Well, suppose the batter hits the ball. He <u>has</u> to run to first base. He has no choice. You could say he is **forced** to run to first. When the next batter comes up, if he hits the ball, not only is he forced to run to first base, but the player on first base is forced to run to second, to make room at first base for the batter.

- When a player is forced to run, so is the player on the base <u>directly</u> in front of him, meaning there is not an empty base between them.

When a force situation occurs, the baseman does not have to **tag** (touch) the runner. He only has to touch the base with his foot, with the ball in his possession, before the runner gets there. I would guess that this rule was made to prevent dangerous collisions at the base since two players <u>cannot</u> occupy one base at the same time.

That is such a "guy thing". Okay, this may be a bit of a stretch, but did you ever notice that when a girl has a (female) friend sleep over, they have no problem sleeping in the same bed? But if a guy has a (male) friend spend the night, you know, say he's too drunk to drive, hell would have to freeze over before they'd sleep in the same bed. Why is that?? One more thing - this is not a marathon. A runner cannot pass the runner ahead of him, and the lead runner has priority to return to the base he started at.

One benefit of a forced out is the **double play** - when two runners are thrown out in one play. For example, say there is a runner at first base. If the batter hits a ground ball, an infielder can glove the ball & throw it to second base, or touch the base himself (depending on how close to the base he is) for the first forced out, then throw it to the first baseman for the second forced out.

There is one situation where a double play may not be attempted, known as the **infield fly rule**. And no, this does not involve insects buzzing around the bases.

- When the batter hits a fly ball that can easily be caught by an infielder, he is automatically out. This is to prevent the infielder from purposely dropping the ball when there is a runner on first base, forcing him to run, creating the easy double play.

So what happens when a player hits a fly ball into the outfield? If the ball is caught, the batter is automatically out. (Remember? One of the 3 ways to retire a batter?) But can the runners advance? There is a way a runner can advance on a caught fly ball - by **tagging up**. That means before he starts running, he must wait, keeping one foot on the base, until the ball touches the fielder's glove. Let's say he thinks the fielder will drop the ball and starts running, but the fielder miraculously catches the ball. The runner must go back to the base he started at, tag up, (touch it with his foot) and can then advance to the next base. That is, if he thinks he has enough time to get there before the fielder can throw him out.

- When there is a runner on base, the batter will often attempt to hit a deep fly ball in an effort to advance the runner. This is known as a **sacrifice fly ball**.

Now, the **tag out** occurs when a runner is not forced to run, for example, a runner at second base when first base is empty. Should he decide to go for it, and take off for third base, the third baseman must tag - actually touch - the runner with the ball. The runner also has the option of going back to second base if he thinks he can make it back safely and avoid the tag there.

Remember how I said base running takes skill, experience, and brains? Well, that's part of it. It also takes good coaching. Just outside first and third base are two (chalk marked) **coaches boxes**, one for the **1st base coach**, and one for the **3rd base coach**. These guys help direct the base runners. When a player is running around the bases at top speed, he doesn't want to have to slow down to see where the ball is. Instead, he relies on the base coach to let him know whether he should keep running or **hold up** (stop) at a base. These calls are pretty much judgement calls the base coaches make based on instinct and experience - for example, how fast is the runner, how good is the defensive player's arm...

Now, there is one situation where the batter must always hold up at second base which is known as the **ground rule double**. This reminds me of a little ground rule I have when it comes to blind dating, ironically also known as the ground rule double. When a blind date turns out to be a complete disaster, make whatever you're drinking a double! But, in baseball, a ground rule double occurs when a ball hits the ground in fair territory and then bounces over a wall making the ball unplayable. It is an automatic double, meaning the batter must stop at second base, and all base runners advance 2 bases.

Sometimes a batter will get an infield hit – the ball stays in the infield – and chances are he won't make it safely to first base. But because of the location of the ball, and the position of the base runners, a fielder may choose to throw out another runner, allowing the batter to safely reach first base. This is known as a **fielder's choice**. He has the choice to throw out the batter or any base runner instead.

THE OFFICIALS

There are four officials, known as **umpires**, in major league baseball; the home plate umpire, the 3rd base umpire, the 2nd base umpire, and the 1st base umpire.

The **home plate umpire** is the "head" official. In conflicting calls, he has the final word. He calls the pitches (balls and strikes) and yells "Play Ball!" to begin the game.

The **base umpires** determine the plays on their bases - for example, whether a runner is safe or out on a throw. But the 1st and 3rd base umpires also make judgement calls on whether a ball is hit fair or foul.

MAJOR LEAGUE BASEBALL

Major League Baseball (MLB) is divided into two leagues, the **American League**, (AL) and the **National League**, (NL). In each league, the teams are divided between 3 divisions; the West, Central, and East. There are 30 teams throughout the U.S. and Canada and are divided as follows:

American League	National League

West

Anaheim Angels	Arizona Diamondbacks
Oakland Athletics (A's)	Colorado Rockies
Seattle Mariners	Los Angeles Dodgers
Texas Rangers	San Diego Padres
	San Francisco Giants

Central

Chicago White Sox	Chicago Cubs
Cleveland Indians	Cincinnati Reds
Detroit Tigers	Houston Astros
Kansas City Royals	Milwaukee Brewers
Minnesota Twins	Pittsburgh Pirates
	St. Louis Cardinals

East

Baltimore Orioles	Atlanta Braves
Boston Red Sox	Florida Marlins
New York Yankees	Montreal Expos
Tamp Bay Devil Rays	New York Mets
Toronto Blue Jays	Philadelphia Phillies

Until recently, baseball was very unique in that it was the only sport that kept its 2 leagues separate until the playoffs. In basketball and hockey, the Eastern Conference plays the Western Conference throughout the season. In football, the American Football Conference plays the National Football Conference. But in baseball, the American League teams only played other American League teams, and National League teams only played other National League teams.

Well, that was then and this is now. Now we have what is known as **Interleague Play**. American League – say hello to the National League because you will now be playing each other. So far it's only the AL West playing the NL West, AL East playing the NL East, and AL Central playing the NL Central, and only 16 +/- games. So it's still a bit experimental, yet very controversial. Long time fans of the game (who call themselves baseball purists) don't like it because they say it takes away from the purity of the World Series where the best from the AL meets the best from the NL for the first time, with no chance of having played each other during the regular season. Now, as for myself, a fan of an American League team, I like interleague play. It gives me a chance to see some of the great players from the National League, whereas before interleague play, I never would have had that opportunity.

There are 162 games during the regular season. Each team plays half of the games at home, and the other half away. At the end of the season, the team with the best record in its division is the division champion.

THE PLAYOFFS

The Major League Baseball Playoffs... otherwise known as the **World Series**. Actually, it's really only the final round between the American League and National League champions that is the "World Series". But nonetheless, to me, the name "World Series" still seems a little glamorized considering it's only played in Canada and/or the U.S., and only between teams from Canada and/or the U.S. So, either I just don't remember the whole world being invited to play, or I missed Geography 101 the day they explained that these two countries make up the majority of the world.

Anyway, the team in each division with the best record (most wins) advances to the playoffs. A **wild card bid** is given to the 4th place team in each league. So that makes eight teams advancing to the playoffs, 4 in the American League and 4 in the National League.

There are three rounds in the playoffs. The teams with the better records get to play the first games at their stadium, known as **home field advantage**. The first round is a "best of five" series, meaning the first team to win three games advances to the next round. The second and third rounds are "best of seven" series, the first team to win four games advancing.

In the first two rounds, the teams play within their own league. In the first round, the division champion with the best record plays the team with the 4th best (worst) record, and the 2nd and 3rd place teams play each other. In the second round, the two winners from the first round play each other, resulting in an American League and National League champion. In the third and final round, (yes, this is what is referred to as the "World Series") the American League and National League champions play each other for the title of Major League Baseball World Series Champions.

And that is the game of baseball.

BASEBALL BLURBS

At Bats - The number of times a player has been up to bat.

Away - The number of outs in an inning - one away equals one out.

Back to Back - Two consecutive hits of the same kind - back to back doubles, home runs...

Bag - A base.

Balk - Failure by the pitcher to complete the delivery of a pitch once he starts the wind-up. The runners advance one base on a balk, and if there are no base runners, the batter gets a called ball.

Ball - A pitched ball that misses the strike zone.

Base Line/Path - The direct path that connects the four bases.

Base on Balls/Walk - When a player advances to first base after receiving 4 pitches that are not swung at, and miss the strike zone.

Bases Loaded - When 1st, 2nd, and 3rd bases are occupied by offensive players.

Batter's Box - The boxes on each side of home plate which designate where the batter must stand while at bat.

Batting Average - The number of hits a batter gets divided by the number of times he comes up to bat.

Batting Order/Line-up - The order in which each offensive player has a turn at bat.

Blooper - A short pop-fly that drops just beyond the perimeter of the infield.

Bullpen - The area in foul territory where relief pitchers practice, and wait to be called into the game.

Bunt - A ball that is tapped only a few feet from home plate, often used as a sacrifice to advance a runner.

Change-up - When a pitcher changes the speed of the pitch to confuse the batter - for example, a pitcher might throw two fastballs in a row, and when the batter expects another fastball, he throws a slowball, intended to mess up a batter's timing.

Check Swing - When a batter starts to swing, but changes his mind and checks (stops) midway through. If he swings less than halfway around, and does not break (turn) his wrists, he is not charged with a strike.

Choke-up - To hold the bat several inches away from the bottom.

Clean-up Hitter - The 4th player in the batting order.

Clutch Hitter - A batter who can be relied on to get a hit when it is desperately needed.

Connect - To hit the ball solidly.

Control - When a pitcher can throw strikes to a specific spot.

Count - The number of balls and strikes on a batter. When a pitcher has more strikes than balls on a batter, he is said to be ahead of the count. When he has more balls than strikes on a batter, he is behind in the count.

Delivery - The act of releasing or throwing a pitch.

Designated Hitter (DH) - A player who bats in the line-up, but does not play a defensive role on the field. Teams in the American League use a designated hitter in place of the pitcher. In the National League, the pitcher bats as there is no designated hitter.

Diamond - The layout of the infield - because it looks diamond-shaped from home plate.

Double - A two-base hit - a hit which enables the batter to reach second base.

Double Play - A defensive play in which two offensive players are thrown out in one play.

Doubleheader - Two games played back to back on the same day by the same teams.

Dugout - The areas along the 1st and 3rd base lines, in foul territory, reserved for the team. Each team has it's own dugout.

Earned Run Average, (E.R.A.) - The average number of runs a pitcher allows, or gives up, during a game. The player may have reached base on a hit or walk.

Eject - To throw a player, manager, or coach out of the game.

Error - A fielding or throwing mistake that allows a runner to advance safely.

doubleheader

Even Count – When the batter has a count with the same number of balls and strikes.

Extra Base Hit - Any hit that is more than a single - a double, triple, or home run.

Extra Innings - The continuation of a game beyond nine innings in order to break a tie.

Fielder's Choice - A hit ball which may be thrown to one base or another for the out - for example, if there is a runner on 1st base and the batter hits the ball to the 3rd baseman, he has the choice to throw to either the 1st or 2nd baseman.

Fair Ball - A ball that is hit between the two foul lines.

Fly Ball/Pop Fly - A ball which is hit high into the air.

Force - When a runner must run to the next base. For example, because two players cannot occupy a base at the same time, the runner on 1st base is forced to run to 2nd to make room at 1st base for the batter.

Foul Territory - The area outside the foul lines.

Foul Tip - A ball that is hit straight back, which the catcher attempts to catch for the automatic out.

Full Count - A count of 3 balls and 2 strikes to the batter.

Games Behind - The number of games in which a team is out of first place. For example, if Team A has 22 wins and 9 losses, and Team B has 21 wins and 9 losses. Team B is half a game behind Team A. If team B has 21 wins and 10 losses, they are one game behind Team A.

Grand Slam - A home run with the bases loaded.

Ground Ball - A ball that rolls or bounces along the ground before a fielder gloves it (picks it up).

Hit - A ball that is hit into fair territory, enabling the batter to reach first base safely.

Hold-Up - When a runner stops at a particular base without attempting to advance.

Hole - A gap, or wide space, between two fielders.

Home Field Advantage – During the playoffs, the team with the better record gets to play at their ballpark.

Home Run - A hit which allows the batter, and all players on base, to score.

Home Team - The team at whose stadium the game is being played.

Infield Fly Rule - When a batter hits a fly ball within range of the infield, he is automatically out. This is to prevent the infield from intentionally dropping the ball, forcing the runners to advance, and creating a double play.

Inning - The period of play in which each team has a turn at bat.

Intentional Walk - When a pitcher intentionally throws 4 balls outside of the strike zone in order to put the batter on 1st base and increase his chances of a double play, or to avoid pitching to a particular batter.

Interleague Play - When an American League team plays a National League team during the regular season.

Lead - 1.) When a team has more runs than the other team, 2.) When a runner gets a head start several feet from the base.

Lead Runner - The runner closest to home plate when there are two or more players on base.

Lead-off Hitter - The first player in the batting order.

Left on Base - The number of players left on base when the team (side) is retired.

Line Drive - A hard hit ball that travels a long distance without rising more than a few feet above ground.

Manager - The leader of a team. He supervises the team, including the coaches; the batting coach, pitching coach, 1st & 3rd base coaches... He puts together the batting order, and makes all substitution and changes in the line-up.

No Decision – What the starting pitcher is credited with when he leaves the game after 5 2/3 innings with the lead, but the team loses the game. This is neither a win or loss on his record.

No Hitter – Due to great pitching and defense, no member of the opposing team gets on base as a result of hitting the ball.

On-Deck Batter - The batter scheduled to hit after the player currently at bat.

Perfect Game - When a pitcher retires 27 batters in a row (3 batters per each of the 9 innings), not allowing any players from the opposing team to reach first base.

Pick-Off - When the catcher or pitcher catches the runner off the base and is able to tag him out before he can get back to his original base.

Pinch Hitter - A player who is called into the game to bat in place of another player.

Pinch Runner - A player who is called into the game to run in place of another player.

Pitchout - A pitch that is intentionally thrown wide, out of the batter's reach. This allows the catcher a greater chance to throw out a runner attempting to steal a base.

Pitchers' Battle - A low scoring game with many strike-outs and very few hits. The game becomes a battle between the performance of the pitchers.

Pulling a Pitch – When a batter takes a full swing, resulting in a hit deep into the outfield toward the side he is batting from. (A left handed batter will hit it to deep left field.)

Put-Out - The act of putting a player out by catching a fly ball or tagging a runner...

Run(s) Batted In (RBI) - When a player scores due to the outcome of the player at bat. For example, a player who hits a home run with a runner on 1st and 2nd would be credited for 3 runs batted in. If the bases are loaded and the batter walks, he is credited with a run batted in.

Relief Pitcher - A substitute pitcher who is brought into the game to replace another pitcher during the game.

Run - One point scored when a player advances around the four bases and crosses home plate.

Rundown - When a runner is trapped between two defensive players, making it difficult to advance to the next base or return to the base he started at. The two defensive players will throw the ball back and forth until one of them is able to tag the runner. (Don't you remember playing "pickle" in elementary school?)

Sacrifice - When the batter hits the ball with the intention of advancing a teammate on base rather than safely getting on base himself - usually accomplished with a bunt or deep fly ball.

Save - The credit given a relief pitcher, usually the closer, when he maintains a lead of 3-runs or less from the time he entered the game.

Scoring Position - When at least one runner is on a base beyond first, and has the opportunity (is in position) to score.

Seventh Inning Stretch - When the fans stand up – to stretch - between the top and bottom of the seventh inning. Yes, this is when you get to sing *Take Me Out To The Ballgame!*

Shutout - When a team prevents their opponents from scoring any runs.

Sign - A secret signal given by a base coach to a runner and/or batter. Also used between pitchers and catchers.

Single - A one base hit.

Slide - An attempt by the runner to get to the base quickly by sliding the last few feet, either by "diving", hands outstretched toward the base, or by "falling" and sliding feet first.

Slump - Poor performance by a player over a period of time.

South Paw – A left-handed pitcher

Steal - To get a head start off base and sprint to the next base as the pitcher is winding up.

Strike - A pitched ball that the batter swings at and misses, hits foul, or crosses the strike zone but is not swung at.

Strike Zone - The area over home plate the ball must go through in order for a strike to be called.

Suicide Squeeze - A play in which the batter bunts to get the runner on 3rd base home. The runner on third base takes off for home plate as soon as the ball leaves the pitcher's hand, and batter must bunt the ball no matter what the location of the pitch is because the runner is already on his way home.

Switch Hitter - A batter who can bat both left and right handed.

Tag - When a defensive player touches the runner with the ball before he reaches the base for an out.

Tag-Up - When a base runner goes back to the base he started at. A runner must tag-up before advancing when a fly-ball is caught.

Triple - A three base hit - a hit which enables the batter to reach third base.

Unearned Run - A run scored as a result of an error.

Warning Track – The dirt along the outfield wall which warns outfielders of the impending wall.

Wild Card – The 4th place team in each league which earns them a play-off spot.

Wild Pitch - A pitch that the catcher misses which results in the runner(s) advancing.

Windup - The motions of a pitcher before he releases the ball.

World Series - The final round in the playoffs where the American League champions play the National League champions.

BASKETBALL

Bounce... bounce... bounce... Up the court, down the court. And back up the court, and back down again. Okay, so it's not brain surgery, but there is more to the game of basketball than you'd think. And knowing a little bit about the different strategies and techniques - shooting, passing, defending - can make the game a whole lot more interesting. And do you want to know a little secret? White men *can* jump.

PLAYING SURFACE & EQUIPMENT

The Court

The playing surface is called a **court**. Now, unlike the legendary courts of Europe, there are no kings or queens, although certain players truly believe they are royalty

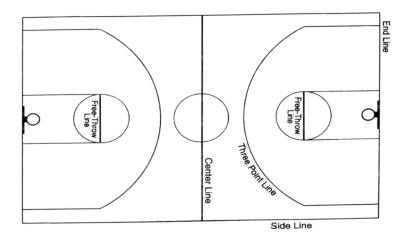

and deserve to be treated as such. The court is often referred to as "the floor", which is divided in half by a **center line**. At the middle of the center line is a 12 foot circle which is used for a jump ball at the beginning of each half. The **basket**, which is 10 feet high, hangs over the **free-throw lane**, also referred to as **the paint**. The free-throw lane runs 15 feet from the end line to the **free-throw line**. The **3 point line** runs from one side of the basket across the court in a semi-circle. Now, there are a few differences between the college game and the NBA (National Basketball Association) in both the rules of the game, and the physical court itself, but I think I'll save that for the end of this chapter.

Basketball is a non-contact sport, and if it looks like a contact sport, somebody's breaking the rules. So no protective clothing, helmets, or extra padding is necessary. Throw on that tank top & long stylish shorts, pull those socks up to your knees, lace up those multi-million dollar endorsement athletic shoes, and you are set. You are a basketball player. Okay, maybe not, but you'll look like one. Besides, I always thought it's not whether you win or lose, it's how you look playing the game.

Now, on the back of the jersey is the players last name and his number, as it is in most sports. The funny thing is, a lot of guys think they have a personal relationship with some of these players just because they know their names and talk to them, through the television, of course. But I guess telling them that these guys are not their buddies, and anyone who can read knows their names, would kind-of be a blow to the ego, which as we all know is sensitive enough.

THE PLAYERS

A basketball team always has five players on the floor at a time; usually consisting of two forwards, two guards, and one center. Some coaches choose to alter the line-up, for example, playing three guards instead of two.

The (2) guards are generally referred to as the one-guard, or point guard/lead guard, and the two-guard, or shooting guard. The **point guard** is the playmaker. His job is to bring the ball up the court and get the ball to the scorers, set up plays, and control the tempo of the game. The **shooting guard**, on the other hand, should also be a playmaker, but he is looked to for outside, or long-range, shooting. He should be able to shoot from any place on the floor (within reason). It kind-of sounds like he should be an employee at a maximum-security prison, doesn't it?

The forwards try to get up close to the basket, to score and to rebound. The forwards are referred to as either the **power forward**, known for his defense and rebounding, or the **small forward** - although I don't know why they're called small, they're anything but - known for his ball handling and scoring ability.

shooting guard

The **center**, usually the tallest player, is essential in both offense and defense. On offense he should contribute to the scoring and rebounding, and on defense he should be rebounding and blocking shots. Kind-of a jack-of-all-trades.

The **sixth man** is the number one substitute "off the bench" who is the first to go into the game when one of the starters comes out.

The **"bench"** is the group of players who back-up the starters. It's not that they're bad players, but the team just has too many good players in a certain position, and only one can start. If he's hot, he stays in. If he chokes, his back-up, from the bench, takes his place. Sometimes the coach just needs to give the starter a rest, or, that starter gets himself into foul trouble. In either case, the starter will take a seat while his back-up (from the bench) goes into the game for him. Teams with a "deeper" bench (more players) tend to have a greater chance of winning games as they give the team more flexibility.

Although each player has a specific job to do, it is essential that everyone be able to score, rebound, pass, play defense, and basically, handle the ball well. When a player has possession of the ball, his entire team is on **offense**. As soon as that team loses possession, or scores, they become the **defensive** team.

THE GAME

The object of the game is to get the ball in the basket. But how that is accomplished is not quite that simple. Why can't a player just run up to the basket and throw the ball in? Why can't the defenders just block and tackle the ball carrier like they do in football? Because that would be too easy, and how much fun would that be to watch?

Play begins with a **jump ball** at center court. The referee throws the ball up in the air as two opposing players jump up and attempt to tip it to one of their teammates. Now you might assume that the team would use it's tallest player, often the center, but that's not always necessarily the case. The best man (or woman on a women's team) for the job is the player who can jump the highest. The other players around the circle cannot move until the ball is tipped.

Whenever you hear a certain team **controls**, it means they have possession of the ball. A player must advance the ball by bouncing it with one hand, known as **dribbling**, as he walks or runs up court. This is not to be confused with drooling, which happens when he sees a gorgeous woman on the sideline as he dribbles up court. And since grabbing or tackling the ball carrier would result in a personal foul, (fouls will be covered later) bouncing the ball gives the defender a chance to knock the ball away.

Once a player dribbles the ball, he cannot stop, and then start up again. He must either pass the ball, or take a shot at the basket. If he were to stop, and then start dribbling again, he would be called for the **double dribble** violation. The one exception is, if a player stops dribbling and an opponent touches the ball and slaps it out of the ball carrier's hands, the player can start dribbling again if he regains possession.

traveling

When a player stops dribbling and carries the ball as he walks, it is known as **traveling**, which is illegal. Just remember, although in life traveling is good, in basketball, traveling is bad. What you will often see is a player using the **pivot** step as a way of turning while holding the ball. One foot is planted, and as they turn on the ball of that foot, the "free" foot can be moved and planted as many times as necessary without "walking", and consequently, being called for the travel.

The Offense

There are basically two ways for the offense to set-up a scoring opportunity. They can "set-up" the play, where the offense takes its time getting into position and runs specifically rehearsed plays. This is designed to get the ball to a specific shooter, at a specific spot on the floor, where he will hopefully be undefended and able to get a clear shot at the basket. The second way is where there is no "set-up", the players just run down the court and pass the ball, hoping one player or another can break free and get an open shot at the basket.

One way this is accomplished is on the **fast-break**. This is where the offensive players quickly get down court and have a shot at the basket before the defense has a chance to set-up. This is usually accomplished with 1.) a defensive rebound, or 2.) a long pass. You know, I'm really starting to believe that for men, sports imitate life, or life imitates sports... just follow my deductive reasoning here. Men often fight for <u>control</u> of a relationship. It starts when, at the beginning, they take the time to plan and <u>set-up</u> a date, but by the 3rd date they just <u>wing it</u> - no thought, no plan, they just go for it and hope they can <u>score</u>. And when they wake up in the morning and panic because they think now she'll want a commitment, they try and make a <u>fast-break</u>, otherwise known as the quick exit. (No, I'm not a psychologist, I just play one in this book.)

Now there are many strategies an offense will use throughout the course of a game, but two of the most common are the **pick and roll**, and the **give and go**, also referred to as the "back door" play. At least these are two that you'll often hear the announcers talking about. I find the "give and go" and the "pick and roll" to be prime examples of the perfect work environment. I would like to <u>pick</u> my own hours so I can <u>roll</u> out of bed sometime around ten a.m., and once in the office, I'd <u>give</u> them a couple of good hours and then <u>go</u> and enjoy the rest of the day. Sounds like employee benefits need some restructuring in my company! But in basketball, both these strategies are where two offensive players work together in an effort to enable one of them to score.

The **pick and roll** is used to free up a player to give him an open path to the basket. A **pick** is a legal block, or a screen, for the player with the ball. Let's say (offensive) Player A is being defended by (defensive) Player X. Player A's teammate, Player B, moves in with the ball and "picks" player X, blocking his view of Player A. Player B passes the ball to

Player A, allowing him to get around (roll) Player X and get a clear shot at the basket. Now, the **give and go** is when Player A passes (gives) the ball to his teammate, Player B. Player A then **cuts** (goes) to the basket and signals to Player B for a return pass, allowing him to score from right under the basket.

Basketball is a very fast paced game, and within seconds, a player must be able to go from playing offense right into playing defense, or visa versa, which is known as **transition**. A team that after scoring can get down court quickly, and immediately set-up defensively, is known as having a good **transition game**. Not to be confused with the floozie your "ex" picks-up after you dumped him. She is his transition fling. Speaking of transitions, I'm going to transition into the defense by first talking about something that is equally important to the offense and the defense, which is **rebounding**. And I'm not talking about the transition floozie your "ex" picked up as a result of being on the "rebound". Just another example of sports imitating life. (Amazing, isn't it?)

So, why is rebounding so important? Because more shots are usually missed than made, and the team that gets more rebounds, known as **out-rebounding** the other team, usually wins. How can that be? You don't get any points for a rebound. True, but an offensive team has the opportunity to get points by grabbing the rebound and taking another shot at the basket, known as an **offensive rebound**. And the defensive team has the opportunity to prevent the offense from getting the rebound, the extra shot, and those two precious little points. (That's right – that would be known as a **defensive rebound**.)

The Defense

Now you know that the offense can pass, shoot, & rebound, what can the defense do to stop them? How does a team keep their opponents from scoring? There are basically two ways a team plays defense; man-to-man coverage and zone defense. And sometimes they'll use a combination of the two.

In **man to man** coverage, each player is assigned one (offensive) player to cover, or guard, and stick with him on the floor wherever he goes. The defense will sometimes "switch" assignments if two offensive players change places, because it is easier, and quicker, for the defense to just change their assignment rather than switch places. The defense will sometimes **press**, meaning they will guard very closely, in an attempt to "pressure" the other team to make a bad pass, lose the ball, travel... in a nutshell, turn the ball over.

A **full-court press** starts when the offense throws the ball in from the end line. Or, you could say it starts when a woman scorned gets a fancy, high-priced lawyer to legally take her "ex" for half of everything he owns. Speaking of... you should see what some of these ex-wives of athletes get for alimony. Let's just say with that kind of money you could buy yourself a nice little beach-front condo on Maui. A **half-court press** starts around the center line. The press is usually "man to man" coverage, and a defender will often leave his man to help a teammate **trap** the ball handler. (But don't be too concerned for him. You know guys, once they start to feel trapped, they'll resort to any means necessary to escape.)

the trap

In the **zone defense**, each player is given a specific area of the floor to cover, and guard whichever players enter his "zone." The center, or other exceptionally tall player, will usually stand near the basket to block shots and grab rebounds. This is also known as **low-post defense**. In the NBA, zone defense is actually illegal. But teams get away with it (usually) by doing some quick shuffling of players.

PASSING

Good passing is key to a team's success. A good pass can open up, or create, a scoring opportunity. There are a number of different passes, but the two most common are the two-handed chest pass and the two-handed bounce pass.

The **two-handed chest pass** is where a player holds the ball with both hands at chest level, and snaps his wrists, putting a **backspin** on the ball. The **two-handed bounce pass** is where the player bounces the ball over to a teammate. Sometimes that teammate is wide open, but there are times when a more skilled bounce pass is required and the player must successfully bounce the ball around a defender. The bounce pass should get to the teammate about waist level, if it's too low it will be hard to reach, and if it's too high it will be too easy to **steal**, which would give the ball back to the other team. Now if those were the only two ways the ball was passed, after awhile it would be kind of boring to watch, and would be more like a game of keep-away rather than one of skill. But lucky for us these guys are extremely talented and can entertain us with more skilled passes, such as:

The **alley-oop (or lob) pass** - This pass is thrown to a player either running down the court or ready to jump up over the rim of the basket. And the timing has to be perfect so the receiving player can catch the ball and either slam dunk it or lay it in the basket all in one motion. Very cool.

The **baseball pass** - Similar to the motion of a catcher throwing to the 2nd baseman, this pass travels a long distance in a hurry. It is commonly used at the beginning of a fast break, but this pass should only be thrown to a player who is wide open as it could easily be intercepted.

The **behind the back pass** - This pass is considered a "fancy" pass, and although some consider it showing off, it is very hard to defend against. This pass usually comes off the dribble rather than a stand-still position. I believe this pass was invented in honor of the athlete who finds his celebrity status justification for overlooking his wedding vows and makes passes at his admiring female fans behind his wife's back.

The **hook pass**- This pass is common when a player is heavily guarded. The player "hooks" the ball around the defender to a teammate.

The **two handed overhead pass** - This pass is also used at the beginning of the fast break by centers or the taller players. The ball is held over the head and the wrists are snapped as the ball is released and thrown over a defending player.

SCORING

Rebounding, dribbling, passing, defending - they're all important skills to have. Now that I think about it, they're very similar to a guy's 4-step program after a break-up: Step 1 - Rebound as fast as possible and find someone new. Step 2 - Dribble over all the available and easy women at the singles bars. Step 3 - Pass on the ones who aren't a sure thing. Step 4 - Defend yourself when you find out she's either married, under age, or a blood relative. But getting back to basketball... Those skills are important, but they don't win games, at least not by themselves. What wins games? Scoring, of course.

A team can score points in two ways; with **field goals** and with **free throws**. Most field goals are worth 2 points, but if a player shoots from outside the 3 point line (both feet are behind it) then the basket is worth 3 points. Each free-throw, that goes into the net, is worth 1 point. There are many different types of shots, and different players excel at different ones. The most common "field goal" shots are:

The **bank shot** - when a player shoots the ball off the backboard, just above the basket, to deflect the shot into the basket. I wonder if this is where the phrase "take that to the bank" originated, considering the kind of "bank" this game earns these guys.

The **dunk** - when a player jumps high enough to get the ball over the rim while it's still in his hand, and "slams" the ball into the net. Just to put this in perspective... you know that the basket is 10 feet high. And I'd say most of the players are between 6 and 7 feet tall - a few are under, a few are over. But even if we take the average player, say 6' 6", we still have over 3 feet to the rim of the basket. Now, jump up in the air. Jump again. How far off the ground do you think you got? 3 feet? Half a foot? It's not easy to get much height, is it? What's my point? I just thought I'd point out that even though it looks easy for a lot of these guys, sometimes I'm just amazed at the heights some of these guys can reach.

dunking

The **hook shot**, or pivot shot - the player's inside shoulder faces the basket as he holds the outside arm fully extended, and shoots over his head and into the basket. (Good form and accuracy probably comes from years of extensive ballet training.)

The **jump shot** - when the player starts with the ball about chest-high, bends his knees, jumps up, and bends his wrists back before releasing the ball. This is the most common shot from 3-point range.

The **lay-up** shot - a shot taken from next to, or in front of, the basket by pushing the ball against the backboard or just over the rim of the net. I know this sounds an awful lot like the bank shot. The main difference is the lay-up is taken from right under the basket, whereas the bank shot is usually taken from a few feet away.

The **set shot** - when the player stops and "gets set", by planting both feet on the floor, and pushing up as he releases the ball.

lay-up

The **tip in** - a rebound tipped in either with the fingers, or kind-of "slapped" in with the palm of the hand.

All of the above shots have one thing in common - there is always a defender trying to keep the ball from going into the basket. And that is where the field goal differs from the free throw.

The **free-throw** is a "free" shot at the basket, from a set distance - the free throw line - without any defensive interference. The "shooter" stands at the free-throw line, while the other players line up on each side of the free-throw lane. A player is rewarded a free-throw when an opposing player commits a foul, which brings me to an important part of the game – fouls and violations.

FOULS AND VIOLATIONS

When a player illegally comes into contact with another player, he commits a **foul**. Some are unintentional, yet some are very intentional. When a player breaks a rule that does not include contact with another player, it is a **violation**. It's very similar to driving a car. You hit another car and you pay a high price, but if you just make an illegal U-turn, the penalty is not quite as severe.

Fouls

A defender can use his body, his arms, and his hands to distract the ball handler, but cannot hold, grab, push, or charge into him. He cannot jump in the way of an offensive player, preventing him from either continuing along a clearly established path, or changing directions. Each time a player illegally comes into contact with an opposing player, he is charged with a **personal foul**. (And if he forgot to put on his anti-perspirant, it would be known as an extreme personal foul!) On the other hand, an offensive player, usually with the ball, cannot run into a defensive player who has established correct defensive position. All that means is that he has both feet securely planted, and the offensive player would be called for the foul known as **charging**. If an offensive player commits the foul, even if he's not the player with the ball, it results in losing possession of the ball to the other team. Each personal foul, regardless of which player commits it, counts as a **team foul**. Team fouls start from zero at the beginning of the second half, but personal fouls carry over. And both personal and team fouls carry over into overtime. The first six team fouls are not shooting fouls. But the seventh, and all subsequent team fouls, result in the "victim" of the foul getting to shoot free-throws. In fact, let me try and clarify the different types of free-throw situations:

• When a player is fouled <u>while he is in the process of shooting</u> a field goal, he automatically gets to shoot a free-throw, regardless of how many team fouls there are. If his original shot goes in the basket, despite being fouled, he gets one free-throw. If his shot did not go in, he gets 2 free-throws if he was attempting a 2-point shot, and 3 free-throws if attempting a 3-point shot.

• On the <u>seventh (eighth & ninth) team foul</u>, the "victim" of the foul gets to shoot a free-throw, even if he wasn't the player with the ball, in what is known as a **"one and one"** situation. If he makes the first one, he then gets a second free-throw.

But if he misses the first, the ball stays in play, and the teams fight for the rebound.

- The players may not move into the free-throw lane until the ball leaves the shooter's hands.

• On the <u>tenth (and all subsequent) team foul(s)</u>, the "victim" of the foul gets to shoot two free throws, regardless of whether or not he makes the first one.

And last, but not least, is the technical foul. A **technical foul** is assessed to a <u>player</u>, or a <u>coach</u>, for one of several reasons; being disrespectful to an official, unsportsmanlike conduct, calling a time-out when there are none left, or an extreme intentional foul. This would be a good time to point out that officials aren't perfect. They're only human, and they make mistakes now and then - but who doesn't?! So, let's say an official makes a call that's a little... wrong. Hey, these guys are going to commit enough fouls as it is, the last thing they need is to be called for one they didn't commit.

So, the player says, *ummm, hey ref, I don't-* and before he can get the rest of the sentence out, he's whistled for a technical. Why? Arguing with a ref. What argument? Exactly! These guys can't sneeze at a ref these days without being called for a technical foul. And, to make matters worse, they can't question it, so they're forced to keep their mouths shut and their aggravation in. Come on, they're guys, they're competing, testosterone's flowing - they need to voice a little frustration now and then. Well, they can't.

So, let's say an offensive player is whistled for a foul which he, of course, disagrees with. Knowing he can't question the ref, it's a waste of breath, he slams the basketball down in frustration instead of handing it over to the ref, and guess what... technical foul. And when a coach gets into it with the ref, well, let's just say there are a lot of coaches who get awfully hot under the collar. If he doesn't back down, he'll get a double technical, and that little tirade will get him ejected from the game. (Otherwise known as premature ejection.)

What is the moral of the story? Don't argue with an official. They're always right, you're always wrong. Gee, is it a coincidence that these "never wrong" officials happen to be... men?! On the bright side, a technical foul doesn't count as a personal foul against that player, but it does count as a team foul. So, what happens to a guy when he gets a technical foul? Well, in the college game, the other team gets to choose their best free-thrower to shoot two free-throws. Then, regardless of whether or not he's made either of the free-throws, his team also gets possession of the ball out of bounds. In the NBA, they only get one free-throw, but they do also get possession of the ball.

What I don't understand about free-throw shooting is why there are very few players who are really good at it. Here a guy is, on the court, with hands and arms and bodies all over him. Well, not all over him, because defending players can't touch the player with the ball, but they can get pretty darn close. So with all this activity and distraction around him, he still manages to get the ball into the basket. But put him at the free throw line, no defenders and a clear look at the target, and more times than not he misses. That is why they say a team's free-throw shooting can either win or lose the game for them.

Violations

A violation is an infraction that results in **turning the ball over** to the other team. It is not a foul, and there are no free-throws, but you turn the ball over enough times and that can make or break a game. In fact, it could be considered a "4 point" turn over - you lose 2 potential points and they have a chance at 2 extra points. Turn the ball over 5 times and that's 20 points you should have had over the other team. You follow? Good!

So, what are all these rules that the players must be abide by? Don't worry, there aren't many. There are two categories of violations, and the first one has to do with the clock: The 3 second rule, 5 second rule, 10 second rule, and the 24/35 second rule.

- The **3 second** rule says that an offensive player can't be in the free-throw lane for more than 3 seconds unless he's rebounding. You might have wondered why the center, often over 7 feet tall, doesn't just hang out under the basket and slam dunk the ball all day long. Well, this is why.

- The **5 second** rule says a team has 5 seconds to get the ball inbounds after they get possession of the ball out-of-bounds, for example, after the other team scores, the ball is knocked out of bounds, or a turnover is committed.

- The **10 second** rule says a team must get the ball over the mid-court line, out of their "defensive zone", within 10 seconds.

- The **24/35 second** rule - 24 seconds in the NBA, 35 seconds in the college game - is the "shot clock" rule. A team must shoot the ball, and at least touch the rim, within 24/35 seconds. If a defender knocks the ball out of bounds, the offensive team keeps possession, they have 5 seconds to inbound the ball, and the shot clock does not re-set. (Isn't the 24/35 second rule what guys learn in high school - that it only takes 24 seconds, 35 seconds with foreplay?)

Then there are the violations for infractions, which are a little more complex than the "clock" violations. Now, many of these terms might sound familiar. So, to alleviate any confusion, the following should help clarify with, 1.) the common everyday definition, followed by, 2.) the basketball related definition.

Carrying
1. What your man does with your bags after he's taken you out for a full day of shopping.
2. When a player dribbles the ball, he cannot hold the ball with two hands at once, or turn the ball over to the other hand while dribbling.

Double Dribble
1. What a guy does when he sees two gorgeous women together (not _together_ together, just hanging out together).
2. When a player stops dribbling, holds the ball, then starts dribbling again.

Goaltending:
1. Keeping an eye on your dreams and aspirations, making sure they're always within reach.
2. _defensive_ - A shot that is blocked on it's way down to the basket. Shots can only be blocked before the ball reaches it's highest point, and if it's blocked on it's way down, the offensive team gets the two points as if the ball had gone in.
   offensive - tapping the ball in off the rim, guiding it in from above the basket. The result is no basket for the offense and losing possession of the ball to the defense.

Lane Violation
1. When an idiot driver cuts in front of you without signalling, causing you to slam on your brakes. (And no, you weren't tailgating, he was just another crappy driver.)
2. When a foul shot is being taken, players cannot move into the lane for the rebound until the ball leaves the shooter's hands. If it's an offensive player, the defensive team gets possession of the ball, and if it's a defensive player, the offensive team gets an extra free-throw.

Out of Bounds
1. When a nosy, busy-body asks personal questions that are clearly none of their business.
2. If a player steps on the line or out of bounds, it results in a turnover. A player can reach for a ball that goes out of bounds if both feet stay inbounds, and "swat" it back into play, but he chances the other team recovering possession of the ball.

Traveling
1. Going on a journey that takes you to new places.
2. Taking more than 1 1/2 steps while dribbling the ball, or when a player picks up dribbling and changes his pivot foot.

THE OFFICIALS

There are two officials on the floor during a college game; a **referee** and an **umpire**, and three for a pro game. If there are any conflicting calls, the referee has the final word. Three officials sit at a table on the sideline; the **scorekeeper**, the **timekeeper**, and an **announcer**, who announces the names of the starting players, and the substitutes when they enter the game.

THE GAME CLOCK

The clock is stopped for fouls, violations, free-throws, time-outs, when the ball goes out-of-bounds, or if an official deems it necessary. A substitute player may only check into the game when the clock is stopped. If at the end of regulation the score is tied, there is a five minute **overtime**. And, if the game is still tied, there is a second overtime, and so on, and so on.., known as double overtime, triple overtime - until the tie is broken. A typical basketball game, without overtime, lasts close to two hours.

THE COLLEGE GAME VS. THE NBA

As I mentioned earlier, there are a few differences between the college game and the NBA. The following should clarify those differences.

The College Game

- It is 40 minutes (of playing time) broken up into two 20 minute halves, with a 15 minute intermission, known as **halftime**.

- Each team is allowed 5 time-outs per half, two **20-second** and three 2-minute, also known as a **full time-out**. There are also four "time-outs on the floor" per half, also known as TV time-outs, because this is when televised games, and radio broadcasts, break for commercials.

- When two players both have hold of the ball at the same time, a **jump ball** is called. The two players used to jump for possession, but now they use a little system known as **alternating possession**. If Team A was last awarded possession of a held ball, the next held ball possession would automatically go to Team B, then back to Team A... Don't ask me why it's still called a "jump ball" when nobody's jumping for it.

- A player is out of the game (he **fouls out**) after committing his 5th personal foul.

- The free throw lane is 12 feet wide.

- The 3-point line is 19 feet, 9 inches from the basket.

- Two free-throws on a technical foul

The NBA

- It is 48 minutes (again, of playing time) broken up into four 12 minute quarters, with a 2 minute time-out between the 1st & 2nd quarters, and the 3rd & 4th quarters, and a 15 minute halftime intermission.

- Each team is allowed one 20-second time-out per half, and seven full time-outs per game. The number of "television time-outs" varies per game.

- When two players both have hold of the ball at the same time, a **jump ball** is called. But in the NBA, they do jump for possession, at the jump circle nearest to where the two players were fighting over the ball. Trust me, this is much more exciting than watching a red arrow light up indicating which team currently has possession, and hopefully some intelligent person will put the jump ball back in the college game.

- A player fouls out of the game after committing his 6th personal foul.

- The free-throw lane is 16 feet wide.

- Zone defense is illegal

- The 3-point line is 22 feet from the basket.

- One free-throw on a technical foul

The NATIONAL BASKETBALL ASSOCIATION

The National Basketball Association, NBA, is divided into two conferences; the Western Conference and the Eastern Conference. Each conference is then divided into two divisions; the Pacific Division and the Midwest Division in the West, and the Central Division and Atlantic Division in the

East. The 29 teams throughout the United States and Canada are broken-up as follows:

WESTERN CONFERENCE

Pacific Division

Golden State Warriors
Los Angeles Clippers
Los Angeles Lakers
Phoenix Suns
Portland Trailblazers
Sacramento Kings
Seattle Supersonics

Midwest Division

Dallas Mavericks
Denver Nuggets
Houston Rockets
Minnesota
   Timberwolves
San Antonio Spur
Utah Jazz
Vancouver Grizzlies

EASTERN CONFERENCE

Central Division

Atlanta Hawks
Charlotte Hornets
Chicago Bulls
Cleveland Cavaliers
Detroit Pistons
Indiana Pacers
Milwaukee Bucks
Toronto Raptors

Atlantic Division

Boston Celtics
Miami Heat
New Jersey Nets
New York Knicks
Orlando Magic
Philadelphia 76ers
Washington Wizards

The number of times two teams will play each other in a season depend on the conference and division they are in. Each team plays a team from the other conference two times, the same conference/other division four times, and the same conference/same division three to four times. For example; the Los Angeles Lakers (Western Conference, Pacific Division) will play teams from the:

> **Eastern Conference** - two times, one game at "home", one game "away".

67

Western Conference, Midwest Division - four times, two games at "home", two games "away".

Western Conference, Pacific Division - three to four times, one to two games at "home", one to two games "away".

The NBA Playoffs

At the end of the regular season, the top eight teams from each conference advance to the playoffs. In the first three rounds, the teams only play within their conference. The first round is a "best of five" series, meaning the first team to win three games advances to the next round. The first seeded team will play the eighth seeded team, the second will play the seventh, the third plays the sixth, and the fourth and fifth seeded teams play each other.

The top four teams with the best records get to play the first games in their arena, known as **home court advantage**. Rounds two through four are best of seven series. The second round is cut down to four teams, two games. The third round, down to two teams, one game, is the conference finals. The two conference champions advance the fourth and final series, where they will play for the title of National Basketball Association World Champions.

THE NATIONAL COLLEGIATE ATHLETIC ASSOCIATION

The National Collegiate Athletic Association, **NCAA**, is broken up into small groups called **conferences**. There are 30 conferences nation-wide, and each conference is comprised of 7 to 16 schools. For example, there is the Pacific Ten (Pac 10) Conference, which is made up of ten schools. Those schools are University of Arizona, Arizona State, UC Berkeley, Stanford, UCLA, USC, University of Oregon, Oregon State, University of Washington, and Washington State. As you can see, those schools are Pacific (Ocean) schools, or close to it. Just as the Atlantic Coast

Conference (ACC) is comprised of schools on the Atlantic Coast...

In college basketball, each team plays 25 - 30 games. And each school plays every team in their conference two times - once at "home" and once "away". The majority of non-conference games are played before conference play starts, but a few are played mid-season. Throughout the season, schools are ranked in two categories; in their conference, and where they stand nationally, only the top 25 teams prominently recognized.

The College Playoffs

The college basketball playoffs are the single most exciting post-season event in sports - college & professional. (And that's not just my opinion - I swear!) It is called the **NCAA Basketball Tournament**, better known as **March Madness**, and it is just that. Two intense action-packed weeks (in March) of single-elimination games in the ultimate quest of reaching the National Championship Game.

In college basketball, making the "runner-up" tournament, the NIT (National Invitational Tournament) won't cut it, and winning the "rivalry" game doesn't hold the same importance it does in football. Everything, all season long, revolves around one thing, and that is the NCAA tournament.

For the top schools nation-wide, nothing short of winning the tournament will do. For the less prominent, yet still competitive schools, their goal is to make it past the first two or three rounds. And I'm sure they always think about being "the one", the one who will pull the biggest upset in NCAA history, and make it to the finals. Hey, they can dream. And for the smaller, unranked (and sometimes obscure) schools, they have just one goal in mind - just getting to the big dance. (Oh, yeah, that's another way this massively important tournament is referred to - the big dance.) Only sixty-four schools will go to the "big dance". Just how they get there is actually a very complicated and difficult process that still confuses me, so in an effort to avoid boring you, I will go straight to the tournament.

The sixty-four teams are broken up into four geographical regions of sixteen teams each; the West, Midwest, East, and Southeast. The number value, or rank, assigned to a team is known as a **seed**. For example, to simplify, the four best teams fill the four number 1 seeds, one per region. The next four best teams get the number 2 seeds... until the last four teams are placed as the number 16 seeds. The number 1 seed will play the number 16 seed, the #2 seed plays the #15 seed, etc. And that is the first round.

Just to get you going on the "lingo", (all the cool kids are using it) the first and second rounds are just that - the first and second rounds. The third and fourth rounds are the regionals, (East regionals, Midwest Regionals...) as they are the last games played solely within the region. And they are referred to as the **sweet sixteen** and the **elite eight**, respectively, as only 16 teams, and then 8, an "elite" group, have made it that far. The fifth round, the semi-finals, is referred to as the **final four**, as only 4 teams, one from each region, are left standing. Midway through the season, "insiders" of the game start talking about the "road to the final four", analyzing and predicting which teams will make it that far in the tournament. The sixth and final round is the championship game, where the last two teams still standing will battle it out for the title of NCAA National Basketball Champions.

And that is the game of basketball.

BASKETBABBLE

Air ball - A shot that completely misses the basket, the rim of the basket, and the backboard.

Alternating Possession - In the college game, during a held ball, the two teams alternate who ends up with possession of the ball.

Assist - A pass to a teammate which results in a field goal.

Backboard - A flat surface that is connected to the back of the basket.

Backcourt - The half of the court with the basket a team is defending.

Base Line/End Line - The line behind the basket that is the end boundary line of the court.

Bench - The group of players who back-up the starters.

Boxing Out - Blocking out an opposing player by standing between him and the basket.

Carrying - When a player dribbles the ball with two hands at once, or turns the ball over between hands while dribbling.

Charging - When an offensive player, usually in possession of the ball, runs into a defensive player who has established proper defensive position.

Defensive Rebound - A ball that bounces off the opposing team's basket after an unsuccessful shot.

Double Dribble - To stop dribbling and then start again.

Double Team - When two defensive players guard one offensive player.

Dribble - To move the ball by bouncing it with one hand while walking.

Fast Break - When the offensive team gets the ball upcourt in an attempt to score before the defense can get back and set-up.

Five-Second Rule/Violation - Players have 5 seconds to inbound the ball to a teammate.

Foul - When a player illegally comes into contact with an opposing player.

Foul Trouble - When a player gets close to fouling out - 5 fouls in the college game, and 6 fouls in the NBA.

Foul Out - When a player is ejected from the game as a result of committing the maximum allowance of personal fouls.

Free-Throw - A "free" shot at the basket, as the result of a foul, from a set distance - the **free throw line** - without any defensive interference.

Free-Throw Lane – Also referred to as "the paint", is the area running from the free-throw line to the end line. It is 12 feet wide in the college game, and 16 feet wide in the NBA.

Full Court Press - When a team defends in the back court as well as in the front court. It usually starts when the offensive team throws the ball in-bounds from the end line.

Give-And-Go - An offensive play where one player passes to a teammate, then cuts toward the basket as his teammate passes the ball back to him.

Goaltending - A shot that is blocked on it's way down to the basket (defensive), or, guiding a shot in, or stuffing it in, while it's on it's way down (offensive).

Held Ball - When two opposing players grab the ball at the same time.

High Post - The offensive area near the free-throw line.

Home Court Advantage – During the playoffs, the team with the better record gets to play in their arena.

Jump Ball - When a referee tosses the ball into the air between two opposing players to start the game. Each player attempts to tap the ball to a teammate. In the NBA, a jump ball is called when two opposing players both grab hold of the ball at the same time.

Key - The area consisting of the foul lane and the free-throw circle.

Lane Violation - When a player moves into the lane for the rebound before the (free-throw) ball leaves the shooter's hands.

Low Post - The offensive area outside the key but close to the basket.

Man-to-Man Defense - When each defensive player guards a specific offensive player.

Offensive Rebound - A ball that bounces off a team's own basket after an unsuccessful shot.

One and One – When a player has to make the first free throw in order to get a 2nd free throw (on the 7th, 8th, & 9th team foul).

Outlet Pass - A pass used to set-up a team's fast break following a rebound or a steal.

Personal Foul - Each time a player illegally comes into contact with an opposing player, he is charged with a personal foul.

Pick and Roll - A legal block used to free up a teammate to give him an open path to the basket.

Pivot - When a player, in possession of the ball, keeps one foot in place while moving and stepping with the other foot.

Playmaker - The player, usually the point guard, who calls the plays.

Screen - When an offensive player blocks a defensive player, without making contact, to give the shooter an open (unguarded) shot at the basket.

Slam Dunk - A shot where the player jumps up above the rim and slams the ball into the basket.

Strong Side - The side of the court where the ball is controlled. If the ball is passed or dribbled across the court, then that side becomes the strong side.

Switch - When two defensive players change "guarding assignments".

Technical Foul - A foul called for arguing with a referee, calling a time-out when there are none left, throwing the ball, a blatant foul, etc. It results in the other team getting one/two free-throws and possession of the ball out of bounds.

Ten-Second Rule/Violation - The offensive team has 10 seconds to get the ball over the center line, which is the line that divides the court in half.

Three-Second Rule/Violation - An offensive player cannot be in the free-throw lane for 3 or more seconds unless they are rebounding.

Throw In - To put the ball into play from out of bounds.

Transition - When a team goes from offense to defense, or defense to offense as the ball moves upcourt/downcourt.

Traveling - Taking consecutive steps without dribbling the ball, or moving the pivot foot.

Triple Double - When a player reaches double figures in three of five of the offensive categories - assists, blocked shots, rebounds, scoring, or steals.

Turnover - When the offensive team loses possession of the ball (to the defense) before they take a shot at the basket.

Violation - An infraction of game rules that does not involve contact with an opposing player.

Weak Side - The side of the court without the ball.

Zone Defense - When each defensive player "defends" a specific area of the court, regardless of which offensive players are there.

FOOTBALL

Many consider football to be the roughest contact sport in the world, requiring strength, speed, skill, and last, but not least, courage. At least I like to think it takes a lot of courage to be at the bottom of a three hundred pound-per-man dogpile, which makes me wonder why a person, typically a man, would voluntarily subject himself to such a brutal, body-crushing, bone-jarring, injury inducing game. (Other than the fact that they make more money in a year than most of us will see in a lifetime.) To the untrained eye, the game of football just looks like a bunch of big guys jumping on top of each other, patting each other on the butts, and dancing & prancing around the field in celebration as if they'd just solved the problem of world hunger or homelessness in America.

Football is a "rehearsed" game, meaning the players attempt to complete specifically practiced, you might even say choreographed, plays. The objective being to move the ball down the field and across the opposing team's goal line by pushing, shoving and knocking the other team down. What makes the game so confusing is, 1) the seemingly technical language that goes along with the game, and, 2) the fact that there is so much going on on the field at one time, it seems too difficult to follow.

Well, as for the "technical" language, most of it is just a bunch of junk that the coaching staffs make up, enabling them to communicate with their players. There are only so many "plays" or strategies out there for teams to use. And if each team used the same terminology, every defense would know what's coming - a running play, a long pass - and successfully keep the offense from scoring. So coaching staffs make up their own terminology so that only their team will know what play is being called. And as for all the commotion that goes on on the field, the solution is simple. Just follow the most important aspect of the game - who has the ball and how far did he get with it.

PLAYING SURFACE AND EQUIPMENT

The Field

The playing field, made of either grass or AstroTurf (fake grass), is 120 yards long and 53 1/2 yards wide. The **goal lines** are 100 yards apart, with two 10 yard **end zones** behind each goal line. (I'm sure you already knew that.)

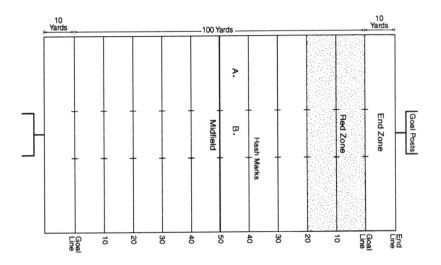

If a play ends here (A), then the next play begins here (B).

Now, down the length of the field are lines that run from sideline to sideline marked at 5 yard intervals. In between the 5 yard lines are short chalk lines, called **hash marks**, which indicate one yard increments. Each play must begin within the hash marks (see diagram). At each end of the field, on the end lines, are upright **goal posts** with a crossbar 10 feet high. They are used for field goal attempts, and after touchdown extra points.

The 50 yard line is referred to as **midfield**. Territory is referred to in terms of the defending team. For example, in a game between the Partridge Family and the Brady Bunch, the Partridge Family is defending end zone "A", and the Brady Bunch is defending end zone "B". The Partridge's 30 yard line is 30 yards from the end zone they are defending, and they will reach the Brady's 30 yard line when they advance the ball 20 yards past midfield (the 50 yard line), and are 30 yards from the goal line the Bradys are defending.

The **red zone** is the area between the opponent's 20 yard line and the goal line. I believe it's called the red zone because it's like a red alert – someone's very close to scoring. If you hear a phrase such as "*the red zone defense is doing a great job*", what they're saying is the defense is doing a great job of keeping the offense from scoring when starting a play from inside the 20 yard line. Just as a good "red zone offense" means the offense is successful in scoring points once inside the 20 yard line.

Equipment

Because of the extreme physical contact of the game, the players wear a lot of protective gear to reduce the chance of injury. You'll notice I said reduce, not eliminate. There are a lot of injuries in football. There are a lot of injuries in all sports for that matter. The players wear a sort of girdle, (yes, a girdle) to protect the lower half of their torsos. (But I think you'd be hard pressed to find a player who'd admit to wearing a girdle.) Up top, shoulder pads are essential considering all the shoulder to shoulder contact. And, actually, second only to the helmet, shoulder pads are the best protection against injury. The helmet has an insulating material inside which acts as a shock absorber by keeping the actual helmet from touching the head, and a chin strap to keep it on. Although, have you ever heard some of these guys being interviewed? I don't know about you, but I think a few of these guys were hit harder in the head than any amount of padding could protect. They also wear mouth guards, elbow pads, wrist guards, athletic supporters, (and no, I'm not talking about cheerleaders) and whatever else they feel will help protect them against injury.

Now, if a guy tells you his <u>football</u> is 11 inches long, and 5 1/2 inches thick, you'll probably be thinking, *yeah, right, that old line*. But you can believe him, because a football is 11 inches long by about 5 1/2 inches wide through the middle (half the length). It also only weighs a little less than one pound. But if he tells you <u>his</u> football is 11 inches long and 5 1/2 inches thick - run!

THE PLAYERS

A team is divided into two "sub-teams", the **offensive** unit and the **defensive** unit, and only one is on the field at a time. When a team has their offense on the field, the other team has their defense on the field, and vice-versa. Each team can have 46 players **dressed**, with 11 players on the field. (Actually, I think that legally, all players must be dressed before they leave the locker room. But the "dressed" I was referring to means being in uniform.) Why so many players on the side lines, you ask? Well, each of the 11 players has a specific job to do, designated by his position. For example, have you seen some of those big players? And I'm not talking about the *strong* big, I'm talking about the *fat* big, although I'm guessing they're pretty strong too. Anyway, I don't think many of them will be breaking any records running a 10K, and they don't have to, because that's not their job. You can be pretty certain that their job is to block.

But getting back to the large number of players on the sidelines... Due to the high rate of injuries, or poor performance, each position must have back-up players, known as **strings**. The best quarterback on a team is the 1st string quarterback. The 2nd best tight-end is the 2nd string tight-end. If a 1st string player is unable to play, the 2nd string in that position, or the next best available, will replace him out on the field.

The Offense

The main objective of the offense, as in every sport, is to score points. The way this is achieved is by moving the ball, using carefully calculated plays, down the field and into the opponents' end zone. Each play, starting the moment the ball is put into play and ending when the ball is called "dead", is known as a **down**. You know what, before I get too far ahead of myself, let's talk a little more about the offense.

The offensive team is divided into two categories - **linemen** and **backs**. Basically, linemen block, tackle, and run interference. Backs handle the ball and attempt to get it across their opponents goal line.

								line of scrimmage
	TE	T	G	C	G	T		WR*
WR				QB				
		RB			RB			

TE – Tight End   T – Tackle   G – Guard   C - Center
WR – Wide Receiver   QB – Quarterback   RB – Running Back

* Also known as Split End

The offensive **linemen** are called linemen because they line up on the **line of scrimmage**. The line of scrimmage is an (imaginary) line that runs parallel to the goal lines, through the ball, and separates the offense from the defense at the start of each play. There must always be 7 offensive players on the line of scrimmage, consisting of 2 ends, 2 tackles, 2, guards, and the center. The paired players can be referred to as "left" & "right", i.e. left tackle, right tackle. The linemen use their bodies to block and hold back the defense. Now they can extend their arms out to hold them back, but they cannot grab or hold them.

offensive lineman

The **center**, in the center of the line, snaps the ball (between his legs with his nice, tight little butt in the air, or more accurately, in the quarterback's face) to the quarterback to begin play. He also snaps the ball back to the kicker and the player who holds the ball on place kicks (don't worry - kicks will be covered later). The center also blocks.

The **guards**, on each side of the center, have the primary job of blocking. They're called guards because in the old days (ask your grandpa), guards were responsible for guarding the center while he snapped the ball. And the name stuck, as did the name of...

The **tackles**, lined up outside the guards, whose responsibility is also to block. And I bet you thought their job was to tackle... but no, they're not allowed to do that. Again, times have changed, job descriptions have changed. You'd think someone could initiate a name change here. Let's see, these five players are the **interior linemen**. I know, how about calling them the interior linemen? (Amazing - I don't even have a PhD!) If this all sounds a little complicated, just remember this one thing - the primary responsibility of the interior linemen is to <u>protect the quarterback</u>.

Now that's just five of the seven linemen. The two players at each end of the line are called... (I'll give you a hint - it's not exterior linemen)... right! **Ends**. And they do their share of blocking, but their primary job is to catch passes. But the two ends have two different names - just to confuse you even more. On the far left, the end lines up right next to the left tackle. He's in there pretty tight, so, he is called the **tight end**. On the far right, the end lines up several yards down from the right tackle. He is still on the line of scrimmage, kind-of "split away" from the rest of the line, so, he is called the **split end**. This doesn't necessarily mean that one end has a great butt and the other has bad hair. Now, just when you thought it couldn't get any more confusing, the split end has a 2nd name - **wide receiver**. His partner is in the backfield, which brings us to the second half of the offensive team - the backs.

The **backs** are made up of the remaining four offensive players; the quarterback, 2 running backs, and a (2nd) wide receiver. They play in the backfield, at least one yard behind the linemen. I'm starting to wonder if they're called backs because they get to stay back while their linemen do all the dirty work on the "battle line"!

The **quarterback** lines up directly behind the center. He receives the ball from the center, on the snap, and has the choice of: a) throwing it, b) handing it off to a running back, or c) keeping it and running with it. You know, a quarterback has to be very secure with his masculinity. After all, how many guys could tolerate having another guy's butt in their face and their hands up in between his legs.

The area in which the quarterback stands, or throws from, is known as the **pocket**. It is about as wide as the two tackles, back to about his running backs. Once the ball is snapped, it sometimes looks as if the quarterback is running around like a chicken with his head cut off. It's because his protection broke down. Now I know what you're thinking, and although I'm sure most of these guys practice safe sex, I don't think they start until <u>after</u> the game. The protection I was referring to is the big, strong linemen who are supposed to hold back the defense, but couldn't, forcing the quarterback to **scramble.** So remember, when you see a quarterback run, it's usually because he is being forced out of the pocket by the defense. This brings me to a couple rules the quarterback must follow. Yes, even though he is the star, just like every other player there are rules he must follow.

When you see the quarterback running, before he gets tackled or runs out of bounds, you might think to yourself, "Why doesn't he throw the ball? There's an open receiver!" Well, the reason is, once the quarterback crosses the line of scrimmage, he cannot throw the ball forward – it would be known as an **illegal forward pass**. And no, he can't run back behind the line of scrimmage and then throw it.

Now, if while he's <u>in the pocket</u> and looking around for a receiver, but none are open, he can't just throw the ball away to get rid of it to avoid getting hit. If he throws it when there's no chance of completing the pass, it is known as **intentional grounding**, and he is penalized. But if he's <u>out of the pocket</u> and he throws it past the line of scrimmage, it is not con-sidered intentional grounding and he will not be penalized. (I seem to recall a couple of intentional groundings after intentionally staying out past curfew!)

The **running backs** run with the ball and block for each other and the quarterback. (Running backs are also sometimes referred to as fullbacks, halfbacks, and tailbacks.)

The **wide receivers** are the fastest runners who can catch long passes.

Now it may look as though there are several players wide open, hopefully on his own team, for the quarterback to throw to. But only certain players, known as **eligible receivers**, are allowed to receive a pass. (As if there isn't already a shortage of eligible men out there.) And they are the tight end, the running backs, and the wide receivers. This means the interior linemen are not allowed to catch passes, or run down field, until the pass has been thrown.

You may have noticed that when the teams are lined up, before the quarterback snaps the ball, there is a player in the backfield who runs parallel to the line of scrimmage, and then back again. No, he didn't have a few too many cups of coffee that morning. He is known as the **man in motion**. All he is doing is trying to confuse the defense. If the defense is using a man-to-man coverage, who will cover the man in motion? Who knows where he will end up, on which side of the field, once the players have sprung into action. Another advantage he has is getting a little jump start, as it is easier to sprint down the field with a running start, rather than from a set, motionless position. Now he can move laterally, or backwards, but he cannot move forward prior to the snap. And he is the only player allowed to move like that, because the rules say that all players on the offensive line, and all but one backfield player, must be "set", perfectly still, until the play begins.

The Defense

As it is the job of the offense to score points, it is the job of the defense to stop them. The defensive team is divided into three parts; linemen, linebackers, and the secondary.

			line of scrimmage
DE	DT	DE	DT
LB		LB	LB
CB			CB
	S		S

DE – Defensive End   DT – Defensive Tackle
LB – Linebacker   CB – Cornerback   S - Safety

The defensive **linemen** are made up of (2) defensive **tackles** and (2) defensive **ends**. As the biggest and strongest members of the defense, they line up on the line of scrimmage directly face to face with the offensive linemen. I guess they have to be pretty strong, considering there are only 4 of them lined up against 7 offensive linemen.

Their most important job is to break through the offensive line, pressure the quarterback, and force him to throw the ball before he's ready. This will result in either an **incomplete pass**, a pass <u>not</u> caught by the receiver, or an **interception**, a pass caught by the defense. Or, if they're fast enough, they can sack him. This is completely different from sacking a woman, which would mean... yep, getting her into the sack. But in football, a **sack** is when the defensemen tackle the quarterback behind the line of scrimmage before he gets rid of the ball, resulting in a loss of yards. (I wonder which one is more fulfilling to a football player?) The linemen are also responsible for keeping the offensive line from breaking through their line.

incomplete pass

The **linebackers** support the linemen by making sure there aren't any "holes" for the offense to run through. They cover the receivers on short passes and make most of the **tackles**, which means bringing the ball carrier down to the ground to end the play. And even though a linebacker has successfully tackled the ball carrier, you'll see several other guys jumping on the pile just for the hell of it – don't ask me why!

The **secondary** - also known as the **defensive backs** - is made up of (2) cornerbacks and (2) safeties. Typically there is one **strong safety**, the bigger and stronger of the two, and one **free safety**, who is faster, and more athletic. The secondary is usually considered the fastest defensemen as they need to be able to backpedal as fast as the wide receivers run forward.

The **cornerback's** first responsibility is to prevent pass completions by covering the eligible receivers, but once the receivers head down the field, they cannot touch the receiver until he actually touches the ball. This includes pushing, shoving, or knocking them down. The cornerbacks also help defend against running plays. The job of the **safeties** is very similar to the job of the cornerbacks, but they are back a few yards deeper, the last line of defense against any loose offensive players on the run for the end zone.

If a defenseman does interfere with the receiver's ability to catch the ball, known as **pass interference**, the pass is considered a completed pass and they will get the first down at that spot. But, on the flipside of the coin, if an offensive player interferes with a defensive player's chance to intercept the ball, the offensive team does keep the ball but is penalized 15 yards from where the play began. Now if an offensive and defensive player catch the ball simultaneously, the offense retains possession.

The defense never really knows for sure what the offense is going to do, well, unless they steal their play book, but sometimes they think they can "read" them. If they predict a running play, the defense would all attack the ball carrier and tackle him within a few yards of the line of scrimmage. And if they think a pass is going to be thrown, they would gang up on the quarterback and sack him before he even got his arm up. In that case, when the secondary gets involved in rushing the quarterback, it is called a **blitz**.

Turnovers

I briefly mentioned that an interception is a pass caught by the defense. What I didn't mention was that an interception gives possession of the ball back to the defensive team. When a ball is intercepted, the player with the ball will run with it and try to get as many yards as he can before he is tackled or run out of bounds. His offensive counterparts will then come onto the field and that is where their first play will begin. Creating turnovers is a big part of the defense's job. They will also attempt to get the offense to **fumble** the ball, where the ball will either fall out or be "forced" out of a players hands. Both teams will scramble to pick up, or fall on, the ball because whichever team comes up with it retains possession.

The following is a typical offensive vs. defensive formation:

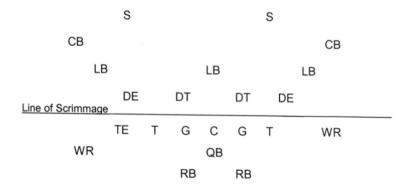

SCORING

There are 4 ways a team can score points:

Touchdown - This is accomplished by running the ball over the goal line, or catching a pass while standing in the end zone (**6 points**).

Field goal - When a place kick goes over the cross bar and between the up rights of the goal post (**3 points**).

Extra point(s) - After a touchdown, with a successful place kick over the cross bar and between the up-rights of the goal post, (**1 point**) or, by running or throwing the ball over the goal line (**2 points**, known as a **2-point conversion**). Why is it that every guy knows this, but most are clueless when it comes to scoring extra points with his "significant other". *What? Make her dinner after I've put in a hard day at the office? What do you mean buy her flowers "just because"?* Yeah.

Safety - When the offensive team carries the ball behind it's own goal line and is tackled in the end zone (**2 points** - for the <u>other</u> team). In this case not only does the <u>defensive</u> team score the points, but their team (their offense) regains possession of the ball.

extra points

KICKING

There are 4 types of kicking situations; the kickoff, the punt, the scoring kick, and the free kick for which **special teams**, or kicking teams (& receiving teams) come onto the field.

The **kickoff** - The ball is placed on a tee - at the 30 yard line in the pros, and on the 35 yard line in college - to put the ball into play at the beginning of each half, and after a touchdown or field goal is scored.

- After the ball travels 10 yards, either team can down the ball, but only the receiving team can run with it.

- If the ball goes out of bounds before the 35 yard line, the ball is put into play at that spot. If the ball goes out of bounds between the 35 yard line and the goal line, the ball is put into play at the 35 yard line.

- If the kickoff goes into or out through the end zone, the ball will be put into play on the 20 yard line. This is called a **touchback**.

The **punt** - A punt is used when the offensive team fails to advance the ball 10 yards and reach another 1st down, and they are not in field goal range, meaning they are too far away to even try. Basically, the punt gives possession of the ball back to the other team without having scored any points. Here's how the punt works. The center snaps the ball back to the kicker, who stands back about 15 yards. The kicker drops the ball and kicks it before it hits the ground, which is known as a **drop kick.**

- Only the receiving team can touch the ball first. But if the receiver fumbles (drops) the ball, anyone, from either team, can pick it up and run with it.

- If a punt goes out of bounds (across a sideline), play will start on the yard line where it crossed the sideline.

- If the punt goes into or out through the end zone, the ball will be put into play on the 20 yard line. What is this called? Right - a **touchback**.

On both the punt and kickoff, the player on the receiving team who fields the punt/kick – known as the **punt/kick returner**, has two options. He can catch the ball, before or after it bounces, and run with it, or, he can signal for a **fair catch** by raising his hand and dropping down on one knee. Once he signals fair catch, the kicking team cannot touch him as the play is then considered "dead" and play begins at the spot of the catch. I happen to think it's a very smart call since he avoids being mowed down by the onrush of defenders running full speed straight at him.

The **scoring kick** - for the extra point - when is this? Right, after a touchdown. The ball is placed on the 2 yard line. The center snaps the ball back to a teammate, who is down on one knee (and you thought romance was dead) and holds the ball for the kicker. For the field goal, the ball is placed at the spot the last play ended. But remember – the kicker stands back about 15 yards behind the center. So a play that ends on the 35 yard line may seem like reasonable field-goal range, but when the ball is snapped back 15 yards, it's really a 50 yard field goal attempt – which is pretty tough.

The **free kick** is used after a safety. The players line up on the 20 yard line and the kicker drop-kicks the ball down field. This isn't a kick you'll see in every game like the others as a safety occurs pretty infrequently.

Oops, I just remembered something I neglected to include here. In fact, although there's going to be a quiz at the end of the book, why don't I throw a question or two in now just for the hell of it. Okay? Great! Let's say a team is down, say by 6 points. They're about to kickoff with just a little bit of time left on the clock, and there is a very small chance they'll get the ball back before time runs out. What should they do? a.) Call it quits and go home, b.) take a time out and go to the locker room to do a quick tequila shot, or, c.) do an onside kick. (I can't believe you said "b"!) The correct, or at least most common answer is "c" - do an onside kick. As you probably noticed, the onside kick is what I neglected to explain.

The **onside kick** is when the kicking team will attempt to keep the ball on their side of the field instead of kicking it to the opposite end zone. Now, the ball must travel at least 10 yards. Since they're lined up on the 30/35 yard line, they will try and kick it just past the 40/45 yard line and attempt to grab, or fall on, the ball before the defense gets it. This gives them the last possession (hopefully) and a chance to score again and win the game. Remember though, the onside kick can only be used after a team scores - either a touchdown or a field goal. Why? Because it must come from a kickoff, and if they didn't score, they would be punting. And that should pretty much do it for kicking.

PENALTIES

Most penalties result in a 5, 10, or 15 yard penalty and a repeat of the down. For example, it is absolutely illegal, and dangerous, for a player to grab an opposing player's face mask. If it is accidental, it results in a 5 yard penalty. If it is deliberate, it is a 15 yard penalty. And, if it committed by the defense, it is an automatic 1st down for the offense. When an official sees a "foul" being committed, he throws a **flag** (a little yellow cloth) in the air. But when a play is in progress, it continues until it is completed. The team who is the "victim" of the penalty has the option to accept the result of the play or have the penalty assessed.

For example, let's say a receiver catches a 45 yard pass, but the defense was called for holding. The offense would most likely decline a penalty on the defense and having to repeat the down, and take the gain of 45 yards and more importantly, the 1st down. But, if the defense was guilty of holding and the receiver dropped the pass, the offense would accept the penalty which would also result in an automatic 1st down at the spot the penalty occurred. Below are a list of the most common "fouls" and resulting "penalties". To ensure that they are not confused with the common, everyday definitions, following each penalty is: 1.) the common everyday definition, and 2.) the football related definition.

FOUL

Clipping
1. Something guys occasionally do to their toenails, like only after they've cut through the front of his shoe.
2. A block applied below the waist to the back of a defensive player other than the ball carrier.

Delay of Game
1. When a guy is late picking you up for a date - after all, dates initially are like games, both "sides" playing perfect people who say and do all the right things.
2. Just what it sounds like - by taking more than the allowed 25/40 seconds to set-up the play, taking extra time for a time-out.

False start/illegal motion
1. Making a move on a woman without her giving the proper "signals".
2. When an offensive player moves his feet, or any sudden movement before the ball is snapped.

Illegal use of hands/holding
1. Being touched or grabbed by someone who makes you cringe.

clipping

2. When the offense grabs or holds a defensive player while blocking. No player can make contact with an opposing player above his shoulders, or shove another player in the back.

Pass interference
1. Kissing another man's woman, or another woman's man. Wait a minute - this is the 90's. So I guess I should also include kissing another man's man, or another woman's woman.
2. The defense cannot touch a receiver, prevent him from catching a pass, more than 5 yards past the line of scrimmage until he has possession of the ball.

Personal foul
1. Wearing dirty, wrinkled clothes, not wearing deodorant, not brushing your teeth or combing your hair.
2. Illegal body contact such as fighting, hitting someone out of bounds...

Roughing the passer
1. Verbally or physically making sure no one cuts in line in front of you.
2. Hitting the quarterback after he no longer has possession of the ball.

THE GAME

The team with the most points wins. There, it's simple, isn't it? Well, it's a little more complicated than that, but the basic principles of the game are pretty simple. The game consists of four 15-minute quarters of playing time, which equals out to be about 3 hours. I know, 4 x 15 doesn't exactly add up to 3 hours. But between scoring, time-outs, and the clock stopping, you'll be surprised how quickly 1 hour becomes 3! After the first and third quarter there is a 2-minute break, the 2 sides switch sides, and play continues exactly where it left off. After the second quarter there is a 15 minute intermission known as **half-time**. No matter who has the ball, and where they have it, that's it. The half is over and when the second half starts, they start fresh. (Although I don't know how fresh they are, I don't think they had time to shower.)

The object of the game is to move the ball down the field in order to score points. But just how that is accomplished is not so easy. The offense is given <u>4 tries</u> to advance the ball (at least) <u>ten yards</u>, from the original line of scrimmage. Remember - each attempt, or play, is called a **down**, starting the moment the ball is put into play, and ending when the ball is called dead. They can either, 1.) **pass the ball** - where the defense will attempt to either intercept (catch) or knock the ball away from the receiver, or, 2.) **run the ball** - where the defense will attempt to stop the ball carrier by either tackling or running him out of bounds. If a player steps on the sideline, he is out of bounds and the play is dead at that spot.

- If a catch is made near the sideline, in the college game the receiver must have <u>one</u> foot inbounds with possession of the ball, and <u>both</u> feet inbounds in the pro game.

Now, they don't have to get those ten yards all at once. Like I said, they have 4 tries to get them, but the ten yards are from the line of scrimmage. So, let's say on the first down the quarterback throws a pass 8 yards, but he **drops back** (takes a few steps back to give himself some room to throw) 3 yards while looking for an eligible receiver. He has only advanced 5 yards, known as a **gain of 5**, because the ball only advanced 5 yards from the line of scrimmage. It is now **2nd and 5**, meaning 2nd down

140! I WEIGH 135! THIS THING'S OBVIOUSLY BROKEN.

gain of 5

95

and 5 yards to go. (That's a good phrase to know.) Now, if the quarterback had dropped back 3 yards and been <u>sacked</u>, it would have been 2nd and 13 - the original 10 yards plus the 3 yards he lost when he was sacked. Remember, if the quarterback throws an incomplete pass, there is no loss of yards, only a loss of a down. But if he is sacked, there is a loss of yards and a loss of a down.

Let's go back to our game between the Brady Bunch and the Partridge Family. This time, the Bradys are the offensive team, and the Partridges are the defensive team. The ball is on the Brady's 20 yard line. Remember, territory is defined in terms of the defensive team. If the offensive team has to cross the 50 yard line to get a touchdown, they are still in "their own" territory.

So, Greg, our strapping young quarterback, passes the ball to the wide receiver, Peter, but as he catches it, he is brought down at the Brady's 26 yard line by the defense. (At least this time Marcia isn't there to get hit in the nose with the football!) He has a gain of 6 yards. It is now 2nd and 4. What does that mean? Right, 2nd down, 4 yards to go to complete the 10 yards. This time, Greg doesn't see any wide receivers open to pass to, so he hands the ball off to a running back, Bobby, who runs but is tackled at the 29 yard line. He has a gain of 3. It's now 3rd and 1 - 3rd down, 1 yard to go.

Now, <u>the 3rd down is very important</u>. If the 3rd down is successful - the offense gets the necessary yardage to complete the full 10 yards - they start over. Four more tries to get 10 more yards. But, if after the 3rd down the offense has not been able to advance ten yards, it is the 4th down and they have 3 options. 1.) They can go for it on the 4th down, 2.) if they are in field goal range, they can go for the three points, or, 3.) they can punt. If they go for it, it's usually because they only need a yard or even less, and they're probably going to try to push their way through. They may pass the ball, but that's not done often. Now if they get it, it's another first down. If they don't get it (the defense holds them back), not only do they lose possession of the ball, but the other team gains possession with good field position. But if they punt, at least they can get the ball deep into the opposing team's territory. *Huh*?! *Like, what did she just say?* Well, let's get back to our game between the Bradys and the Partridges.

We left off with the Bradys on their 29 yard line, 3rd and 1. Greg, our quarterback, throws a pass to Peter, the wide receiver, but Peter drops it. Remember, an incomplete pass results in a lost down but no loss of yards. So, now it's 4th and 1. They are on their own 29 yard line, which would make it an 81 yard field goal (21 yards to the 50 (midfield), and 60 yards to the end line). It won't happen. Trust me, the <u>average</u> field goal is about 35 yards.

So, they've determined they're out of field goal range, leaving them with two options. If they go for it and make it, it's 1st and 10. That is known as a **fourth down conversion**. They've "converted" that 4th down into another 1st down. Just as if they complete the 10 yards on the 3rd down, that would be a 3rd down conversion. (Next time you're watching a game with your guy, when your team is on it's 3rd down, ask him if he thinks they'll be able to convert. What? You've never seen him speechless before?)

Now, if they decide to go for it and don't make it, well, that's not good. *Why,* you ask? Because now the Partridge's offensive team and the Brady's defensive team will come onto the field, (remember, they only get 4 chances to make the ten yards) and guess where the Partridges get to start their drive. (No, not in that big, multi-colored bus.) A **drive** is the offensive team's total consecutive plays in their attempt to score. So, where are the Partridges going to start their drive? Right - at the place the Bradys left the ball after their 4th, and failed, down - at the Brady's 29 yard line. The Partridges only have 29 yards to go to reach the end zone and score. If they don't get the touchdown, they are definitely in field goal range. And that is why teams usually choose to punt in 4th down situations. When a team punts, they have a chance to kick the ball all the way downfield, deep into the other team's territory. So if the Bradys punt and are successful getting the ball deep, that's where the Partridges will have to start their drive.

If at the end of 60 minutes of play the score is tied, the game goes into **overtime**. In the pros (NFL), overtime is 15 minutes long, and the team who scores first wins. If neither team scores, the game ends in a tie. (In the playoffs, there is no tie and they play until someone scores.) A coin toss determines which team will receive first. The defensive team will kick off from the 30 yard line, the same place from which they kick off in regulation. Their job is not only to stop the offense from scoring, but to keep them deep in their own zone. That way, if the offense has to punt, it will give the defense good field position. I know it doesn't sound real fair, that the team who receives the ball first is probably going to be the team to score first. But the defense, more often than not, stops the offense, giving their team the chance to win. Now, if you prefer an overtime that gives each team more of an equal chance to score, then you will like the college game's version.

In the college overtime, each team gets a chance to score starting on the 25 yard line, 25 yards from the end zone. The same end of the field is used for both teams. They have the usual four downs to either score a touchdown, get another 1st down and try again, or make a field goal. And after both teams have gone, whoever has more points wins. (As many overtimes are played as necessary until one team breaks the tie.) But here's why the team that goes 2nd has a slight advantage.

Let's say the Bradys go first, as determined by a coin toss, they can't convert (remember that one?) and are on the 4th down. They'll need a touchdown in case the Partridges get a touchdown. But if they go for it and are stopped, they get no points. Zero. Zilch. And then all the Partridges would need to win is a field goal, which they can probably make from the 25 yard line, on their first down. But, if the Bradys settle for the field goal, and the Partridges are stopped on the 4th down, they can either tie it with a field goal, and go to the 2nd overtime and start all over, or go for the touchdown. If they get it, they win. If they don't get it, the Bradys win.

THE OFFICIALS

There are seven **officials** on the field during the game. And although each official has the authority to make any call at any time, at any place on the field, the referee is the top official. If there are any conflicting calls, the referee has the last word. You know, I have to admit, I don't really know a lot about these guys. Where did they get their training? What makes them qualified to do this job? Well, instead of researching this bit of information, I decided to just go with my astute observations of what seems to be the primary qualifications for the job of professional sports official. What are some of my perceptive observations?

Well, to be an official in the NFL, you must be... OLD! Swear to God, those guys are all at least 80 years old. Oh, all right, I'll tell you one more. To be an official in major league baseball, you must live on a strict diet of... fast food. And only fast food, with a minimum of 3 meals per day. And if you decide to have an in-between meal snack, it must consist of at least one of the 4 major food groups - fat, salt, sugar, or cholesterol. As I said, it's just an observation...

THE CLOCK

As if the game isn't complicated enough, there is one more technicality I need to explain, and that is the clock. Now, there are two clocks you need to be aware of. There is the game clock, which is 15 minutes per quarter of playing time. And then there is the play clock, which helps to keep the game moving along at a smooth pace.

The **game clock** starts to run when the ball is kicked - except, after the two minute warning, the clock starts when the ball is touched by the receiving team. During the game, when a play is over, the game clock keeps running, unless, 1.) there's an unusually large pileup and the referee has to stop the clock to help the players "untangle" themselves, or, 2.) one of the following occurs:

- The ball/ball carrier goes out of bounds
- An incomplete pass
- Either team scores
- A penalty is called
- After a kick the receiving team allows it to roll dead
- A touchback
- Time out is called (each team is allowed 3 per half)

Actually, each team is allowed to call 3 time-outs per half, but sometimes the officials will need to call a time-out. Why? Well, for example, when it's a close call of whether or not the offense has reached the necessary yardage to get the 1st down, it may be necessary to measure the <u>exact</u> yardage gained with chains. (No, not the 25 pounds of chains & jewelry around the players' necks.)

The **chain** is 10 feet long with a "marker" at each end. One marker is placed where the ball was on the last first down, and is stretched it's full length. If the ball is between the two markers, it has not reached the 10 yards, and it is not a first down. But if any part of the ball is beyond the point where the chain ends, it has (at least) the necessary ten yards, and it is another first down. (Every time a first down is made, the chains are moved.) And because it takes time to move the chains and measure the yardage, the clock is stopped. (The guys who come running onto the field with the chains are sometimes referred to as the chain-gang.)

Then there is the **play clock**. This is what keeps the game from lasting 6 hours. As play continues and the official puts the ball in play, the offense has 40 seconds to start their play.

If the clock was stopped, the offense has 25 seconds to start their play. This includes the **huddle**, which is the thing that kind-of looks like a group hug where the quarterback relays the play (called by the coach) to his teammates, to snapping the ball. As it gets close to the end of the game, the team that is ahead will try to run the clock down by using the full 25/40 seconds and running without going out of bounds. The team that is behind will try to stop the clock by running out of bounds and using their remaining time-outs. When two minutes remain at the end of each half, the referee calls a time-out, known as the **two-minute warning**. This short break helps both the offense and the defense plan their strategies to either hold the lead, or get the lead. (Although many men believe the two minute warning, at the end of the 2nd half, is to let them know the concessions stand is about to stop serving beer.)

The NATIONAL FOOTBALL LEAGUE

The National Football League, **NFL**, is divided into two conferences; the American Football Conference, the **AFC**, and the National Football Conference, the **NFC**. These two conferences are each broken down into three divisions; Eastern, Central, and Western. The 30 teams that make up the NFL are divided among these divisions as follows:

<u>AFC</u>   <u>NFC</u>

West

AFC	NFC
Denver Broncos	Atlanta Falcons
Kansas City Chiefs	Carolina Panthers
Oakland Raiders	New Orleans Saints
San Diego Chargers	Saint Louis Rams
Seattle Seahawks	San Francisco 49ers

AFC	**NFC**

Central

Baltimore Ravens	Chicago Bears
Cincinnati Bengals	Detroit Lions
Jacksonville Jaguars	Green Bay Packers
Pittsburgh Steelers	Minnesota Vikings
Tennessee Oilers	Tampa Bay Buccaneers

East

Buffalo Bills	Arizona Cardinals
Indianapolis Colts	Dallas Cowboys
Miami Dolphins	New York Giants
New England Patriots	Philadelphia Eagles
New York Jets	Washington Redskins

No, there isn't a typo, and no, nobody failed geography 101. And although it appears as if a few of the teams are in the wrong division, such as the Arizona Cardinals and Atlanta Falcons, that is the way they are divided up. You see, sometimes a team will move to a new city. They will just up and move in the middle of the night. Okay, not exactly in the middle of the night, they probably do wait for daylight. And when a team relocates, it remains in it's original division. I would guess it's to keep the conference alignment even, although it probably makes the extra traveling a pain in the butt!

There are 16 games during the regular season; 8 games will be played at home, and 8 games will be played away. There are 17 weeks of actual games, but each team gets one week off known as a **bye**. In football, there are several variables which determine the number of times 2 teams will play each other. But to simplify, the league can basically be divided into two parts - a team's own division, and the rest of the NFL.

A team will play the teams in it's own division 2 times - once at home, and once away. As for the other divisions, the main determining factor is how a team ranked the previous season. The teams with the best records will have the toughest schedules the following year, just as the teams with losing records will have easier schedules. How a team does in the post-season (the playoffs) plays a part in determining their schedule for the following year.

NFL Playoffs

You may have heard of a little thing called the **Superbowl**. And although it occurs on the last Sunday of January, men usually start preparing sometime late August, early September, inviting the guys over, stocking up on pretzels and beer... And it'll probably be marked down on his calendar before your birthday and anniversary, but it's not entirely his fault. Only a few weeks of football go by and professionals in the industry start making their early predictions of which teams will be there. The superbowl testosterone is then automatically released in all men. It's totally hormonal, kind of like PMS. We know it's coming, but there's nothing we can do about it.

So, just how does a team make it to the superbowl? 12 out of 30 teams advance to the playoffs. The top team from each division automatically clinch a play-off bid. The other 6 teams get there by way of a **wild card bid**. A wild card bid goes to the next 3 teams with the best record in their conference. Those 3 teams could all be from the same division, or from different divisions. The 2 teams with the best records in each conference get to skip the first round of the playoffs. So in the first round, the third place division winner plays the #3 wild card team (the wild card team with the worst record), and the #1 and #2 wildcard teams play each other.

The playoffs are single game elimination, meaning you lose one and you're free to go practice your golf game. You win and you move on to the next round. In fact, football is the only professional sport whose playoffs are single elimination. The other three are made up of rounds of "best of" series, i.e. best 3 out of 5, or 4 out of 7 games per round. The winners of the two conferences advance to the superbowl - the brass ring, the big banana, the main event in professional football. It determines which team reigns supreme and has bragging rights for one year, until the next superbowl, as the best team in professional football. Did I mention the commemorative superbowl championship diamond ring the winners get, in addition to a big, fat bonus?

THE NATIONAL COLLEGIATE ATHLETIC ASSOCIATION

The National Collegiate Athletic Association, **NCAA**, is broken up into small groups called **conferences**. There are 30 conferences nation-wide, and each conference is comprised of 7 to 16 schools. For example, there is the Pacific Ten (Pac 10) Conference, which is made up of ten schools. Those schools are University of Arizona, Arizona State, UC Berkeley, University of Oregon, Oregon State, Stanford, UCLA, USC, University of Washington, and Washington State. As you can see, those schools are Pacific (Ocean) schools, or close to it. Just as the Atlantic Coast Conference (ACC) is comprised of schools on the Atlantic Coast. This should start to sound familiar if you've read the chapter on basketball.

The number of games each team plays differs with each conference. For example, in the Pac-10, each team plays 8 of the remaining 9 schools. In the place of the 9th school, the team gets the week off, known as a **bye**. In the Big-12 Conference, each team only plays 8 of the other 11 schools. In the place of the other 3 schools, each team will either have a bye, or play a school from another conference. Most schools play their non-conference games before conference play begins.

College Bowl Games

When it comes down to it, only two things matter in college football - being the national champions, and getting to, and winning, a bowl game. Actually, three things matter, the 3rd being winning big rivalry games. Every conference has one, and for some, winning that game can be even more satisfying than going to a bowl game. Some of the biggest rivals are USC – UCLA, Texas – Texas A&M, Michigan - Ohio State, University of Florida - Florida State, and Army - Navy, to name just a few. But there are dozens of others.

Throughout the season, schools are ranked in two categories; in their conference, and where they stand nationally. The **national rankings**, only the top 25 schools prominently recognized based on their overall record, determine which schools will be in the running to play in the *National Championship* **bowl game**. Aside from the national championship game, there are several other bowl games that are very prestigious and recognize the outstanding schools around the country. The **conference rankings** help determine which schools will go to a bowl game, based solely on a team's conference record. So, just how does a school get to a bowl game? Well, at the end of the season, schools are invited to participate in bowl games by sponsors of the bowl. Now the more prominent, prestigious bowls are reserved for the top, most competitive conferences, and the top schools within them. But in many conferences, the second and third place teams are invited to participate in a bowl game as well. And for the schools that don't have a reputation as a ranked, top football program, the bowl games, even the less prestigious ones, bring them national recognition and help their recruiting for years to come.

And that is the game of football.

FOOTBALL FAVORITES

Blitz - When one or more linebackers and defensive backs charge through the offensive line in an attempt to sack the quarterback while he is still in possession of the ball.

Bye – The week(s) a team has no game scheduled during the regular season.

Clipping - A block applied below the waist to the back of a player other than the ball carrier.

Completion - A pass that is legally caught.

Down - An offensive play that begins when the ball is snapped and ends when the ball becomes dead. A team has four downs to gain 10 yards, and earns a first down every time that 10 yards is achieved.

Extra Points - After a touchdown, one extra point can be earned by kicking the ball through the goal posts, and two points earned by throwing or running the ball into the end zone.

Fair Catch - After a team punts the ball, a defensive player signals fair catch by raising his hand, indicating he will not run the ball. Just as after signaling fair catch a player may not run with the ball, he also cannot be tackled.

Field Goal - 3 points earned when a place-kick goes through the goal post from the spot the ball was at (usually) after an unsuccessful third down was completed.

Field Position - The location at which a team has the ball on the field in relation to reaching the opponents' end zone.

Formation - The way in which a team lines itself up on the field at the beginning of each play.

Fumble - A ball that is dropped or otherwise becomes loose.

Hail Mary – Slang term for a last second, very, very long (almost desperate) pass intended to score a touchdown.

Handoff - When the quarterback hands the ball off to a teammate.

Hang Time - The number of seconds in which a kicked or punted ball stays in the air.

Hash Marks - Short chalk marks in between the 5 yard lines to indicate 1 yard increments. A play must begin inside the hash marks.

Holding/Illegal Use of Hands - When an offensive player grabs and holds onto a defensive player while blocking.

Home Field Advantage - During the playoffs (NFL), the team with the better record gets to play at their home stadium.

Incomplete Pass - A pass that is not caught by the intended receiver.

Intentional Grounding - When the quarterback throws the ball from inside the pocket to where there are no eligible receivers in order to avoid the sack.

Interception - A pass that is intended for an (offensive) receiver but is instead caught by a member of the defensive team, turning possession of the ball over.

Kickoff - A place kick used to begin play at the beginning of the half or after a team scores.

Lateral Pass - A pass thrown along or behind the line of scrimmage.

Line of Scrimmage - An imaginary line through the ball that separates the offense and defense at the beginning of each play.

Offsides - A five yard penalty to a team for crossing the line of scrimmage before the ball is snapped.

Onside Kick – When the offensive kicking team attempts to keep the ball on their side of the field instead of kicking it to the opposite end zone. The ball must travel at least 10 yards for the kicking team to be able to recover it. When a team is behind, this gives them the last possession (hopefully) and a chance to score again and win the game.

Pass Interference - Illegally impeding a player's opportunity to catch or intercept a pass.

Pass Rush - When the defense attempts to tackle the quarterback before he can pass the ball.

Penalty - The punishment for an infraction, resulting in loss of yards and or the loss of a down.

Pitchout - Tossing the ball laterally or back to a receiver.

Place-kick - A kick made while the ball is either held by a teammate or placed on a tee.

Pocket – The area behind the offensive linemen, between the two tackles, where the quarterback stands to pass.

Punt - A kick made by dropping the ball and kicking it before it touches the ground. Used after a team is unable to get the necessary 10 yards for a 1st down, and are out of field goal range.

Punt Returner - The player that fields the punt on the receiving team.

Recover - To gain possession of a fumbled ball.

Red Zone - The area between the (opponent's) 20 yard line and the goal line.

Rushing - Running with the ball on a play from the line of scrimmage.

Sack - To tackle the quarterback behind the line of scrimmage, for a loss of yards, while he is still in possession of the ball.

Safety - Two points awarded to the defense when they force the offense to go down (be tackled) in their own end-zone.

Snap - The action of the center handing the ball back, between his legs, to the quarterback or punter.

Special Teams - The players that are on the field during a kicking situation; the kickoff, the punt, and scoring kicks.

Touchback - When a kick goes into or out through the end zone, the ball will be put into play on the 20 yard line.

Touchdown - Six points earned by catching the ball, or running the ball into the end-zone.

Trap - A blocking play by the offensive team in which they allow a defensive player to run to a certain point before they block him from all directions.

Two Point Conversion - After a touchdown two points can be earned by successful throwing or running the ball into the end zone.

ICE HOCKEY

"I went to a fight and a hockey game broke out". Sound familiar? This is not an uncommon perception of the game by people who have yet to learn, enjoy, and fully appreciate the game of hockey. Not to say there isn't a fair share of fighting, but once you learn to love the game, you'll see it's only a small part of what makes hockey one of the most exciting, intense, and addictive sports around.

PLAYING SURFACE AND EQUIPMENT

Ice hockey is undoubtedly "the fastest game on earth", probably because it's not played on "earth", but on ice. This allows players to reach speeds of fifty five miles per hour, and the puck up to twice that fast.

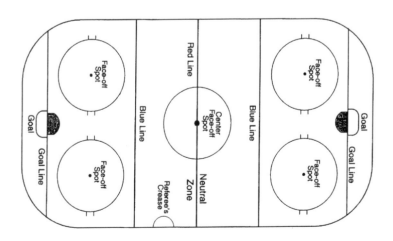

The Rink

In hockey, the playing surface is called a rink, but is generally referred to as the **ice**. It is surrounded by a wall, called the **boards**, which are approximately three feet high. They enable the puck to stay in play most of the time instead of sliding out of bounds each time a pass between players is missed. (Which is pretty often, so these boards prevent the games from being 5 to 6 hours long!) Two **blue lines** divide the ice into three equal parts known as **zones**. The three zones are the **offensive/attacking zone**, the **neutral zone**, and the **defensive zone**. The rink is also divided in half by a center line, known as the **red line**. And they are called the red/blue lines because they are painted red/blue. Not exactly imaginative, but it helps to keep things simple. There are five **face-off circles**, two in each defensive zone, and one at center ice. The **goal** is six feet wide and four feet high. The **goal crease**, the light blue area in front of the goal, is eight feet wide. The goaltender will stand in the crease while protecting his goal.

The Equipment

The **puck**, used instead of a ball, is a hard rubber disk, three inches across and one inch thick. But don't let the "rubber" part fool you - it could knock a guy unconscious. It is pushed around the ice, and into a goal, by a **stick**, which is shaped like a slightly distorted "L".

The players, obviously, wear skates. But they don't wear the kind with those "claws" at the front end of the blade. Those are for figure skaters, and they use them to stop. But see, the reason hockey players don't need them is because the way they stop is by slamming into the boards at full speed. And the way they cushion the impact is by making sure they have an opposing player between themselves and the boards. Now, the skates not only allow them to move around quickly, but to gain a lot of momentum, which could lead to serious injuries. That is why the players wear protective clothing as well as helmets fastened on with a chin strap.

You know, it used to be so easy to tell hockey players apart from other athletes. They were the ones with missing teeth and broken noses. But I guess that's out of fashion now as many players opt to wear visors to protect their face. Goaltenders wear a full face mask, and twice the padding and protective gear as the other players. Then again, wouldn't you if you were on the receiving end of a puck being shot a hundred miles an hour from close range?! The uniform itself is also unique. Did you ever play the word association game? You know, up - down, hot - cold, broken - heart... Well, when I hear the word preppy, hockey players don't exactly come to mind. But for some reason hockey players prefer that their jerseys be referred to as sweaters. Although I'm sure if they had collars, they wouldn't be worn up!

THE PLAYERS

Each team is allowed only 20 members of the team to play in each game, which must include a starting and back-up goaltender. The players who don't participate in a game are known as **scratches**. Only six players can be on the ice at a time, and those players are three **forwards,** two **defensemen**, and a **goaltender**. The forwards consist of a **left wing**, **right wing**, and **center**, who plays between the two wings. And no, their positions don't reflect their political beliefs. In fact, I'm quite sure there are many right wings who are pro-choice and believe in welfare reform, just as I'm sure there are many left wings who want to lower taxes and are anti-gun control.

Hockey is very similar to basketball in that each player takes on both an offensive and defensive role depending on who has possession of the puck. And although you will see players all over the ice during any given shift, each player does have a role to play as designated by his position, and by what his strengths are. Some forwards have exceptional speed, some have exceptional power. There are forwards who are great at scrapping for the puck in the corners and along the boards, who are known as being scrappy little players, which is a good thing, I think. And then there are those forwards who have the job of staying on the opponent's "star player" to keep him from getting a clear shot on goal. It's kind-of like having a shadow on you at all times, which I can imagine would be really annoying, which is probably the point.

Now the center is kind-of the "leader of the pack". He directs play in both the offensive and defensive zones. And he is the guy you'll usually find in the face-off circles - face-offs are his specialty. Not like in the movie "Face-Off" where John Travolta and Nicholas Cage rip their faces off and exchange them – that was really weird. Although in hockey, I can't guarantee you that a player's face will stay completely in tact. But hockey isn't all broken bones and bloody noses. In fact, in recent years, it really has become a game of skill and finesse. Really! (Don't worry – I'll get to face-offs in a minute.)

So, as you can see, there are many roles the forwards play, with many responsibilities out on the ice. But the most important, the main reason they're out there in the first place, is to score. (What guy isn't?!) And there are many "offensive-minded" defensemen on each team, meaning they like to play up in the offensive zone and create scoring opportunities. But their job, first and foremost, is to be a defenseman, to help the goaltender protect the net and prevent the other team from scoring. When an initial shot on goal is taken, it is the goaltender's responsibility to keep it out of the net, any way he can. But if the puck stays in play, and there is a rebound opportunity for the offense, it is then the defenseman's job to clear it as far away from the goal as possible.

Let me back up there for a second. I just briefly touched on the phrase **shot on goal**, which can, and does, lead to some confusion to just what constitutes a shot on goal. One of the most obvious concepts, which sometimes tends to elude some of the players, is that if you don't shoot the puck, you're not going to score. Now it may look as if shots are constantly being taken at the goal, but half of them don't count as a shot on goal. The reason is, to be considered a shot on goal, the puck must either 1.) go into the net, or 2.) be directed to the net with intent to score, and be played by the goaltender. The latter meaning the goaltender must catch, deflect, smother, kick - basically, somehow make contact with the puck, and prevent it from going in the net.

Now if a player shoots the puck towards the net, but the goaltender plays it <u>outside</u> the net, say he sticks his skate out and deflects it, would it count as a shot on goal? Here's how you can tell. Had the goaltender not been there, would the puck have gone into the net? So, if it's shot wide of the net, and the goaltender deflects it, it still does not count as a shot on goal. It's just like when a guy hits on a girl and she shoots him down. Do you think he counts it as a "shot at girl"? Heck no! He only acknowledges hitting on the girls from whom he gets some kind of "contact" out of. No contact, no attempt (shot) taken.

Throughout the course of the game, it will appear as though players are coming and going onto and off the ice at their own leisure. Skate a few minutes, take a break. Well, believe it or not, this is a carefully calculated maneuver by the coach. Because of the fast and physical pace of the game, the players can't stay on the ice for long periods of time. Before the game, the coach will determine which forwards are playing well together, and put them on the ice as a **line**. Just as he will pair up defensive units to play together. Most teams play 4 lines, with the most talented forwards usually playing on the first line. So, when you hear a team is making a **line change**, it is just that. One line will go off the ice, and rest, as a new line goes on. The time a player is on the ice is known as a **shift**. Forwards are typically on the ice for two minutes and off for four, and defensemen are on for three and off for three. During the game, a coach might mix up the lines several times before he finds one that clicks and is successful together. One night a line may play extremely well together, and the next, they're totally out of sync and need to be paired with other players. Now that I think about it, it's kind-of like a celebrity marriage. One day they're happy and in love, and before the next holiday they've decided they're not compatible and are exchanging *till death - I mean, till the next holiday do we part...* with other celebrities' "ex's".

THE GAME

The game is divided into three 20-minute **periods** of play, with a 15 minute intermission between periods. The clock stops for all penalties, violations, time-outs, goals scored, face-offs, and when the puck goes out of play. This translates to approximately 45 minutes per period. If at the end of sixty minutes of play the score is tied, there is a five minute **overtime**. Overtime ends as soon as someone scores the tie-breaking goal. If at the end of five minutes neither team has scored, the game ends in a tie. In fact, hockey is one of the two professional sports that can end in a tie. What is the other one? Right – football. As for the other two, basketball & baseball, they keep playing until one team wins.

Play begins with a **face-off** at center ice. The face-off is at center ice at the beginning of each period and after a goal is scored. A player, remember - usually the center, from each team stand squarely opposite each other, facing his opponent's goal. The blades of the stick must be on the ice, and the referee drops the puck on the ice between them. A player will try to win the face-off by getting the puck back to one of his teammates. A face-off will take place in one of the neutral-zone or end-zone spots whenever play stops for any reason besides a goal scored.

For example, if a puck goes flying over the boards into the crowd, no matter which team sent the puck over the boards, the face-off will take place at the face-off circle nearest to where the puck went "out of bounds". But each team will do everything it can to keep the face-offs in their offensive zone. For example, while in play, the puck may be kicked or batted down with a glove without stopping play. If while fighting for the puck it gets pinned to the boards, by sticks or skates, a face-off is called. The offense will sometimes intentionally create this situation if the puck is in their attacking corners, because it will force a face-off, which can lead to a scoring opportunity.

Often when a team is down by one goal with less than a minute left to play, they will take their goaltender out (**pull the goalie**) and put an extra attacker (skater) on the ice. This leaves an open goal at their own end. But the reasoning is if you can't tie the game with the extra attacker, it doesn't matter if the other team scores (an **empty net goal**) because the game is over. If you do score, you can put the goaltender back in, and usually go to overtime.

<u>Goals and Assists</u>

A **goal** is scored when the puck crosses over the goal line between the posts and under the cross bar of the goal. A puck cannot be kicked into the goal, but, if a player from the attacking team hits the puck with his stick and it deflects off the skate of a player into the goal, the goal counts. Yep, even if it's off a defensive player's skate. Now, there aren't too many rules regarding goal scoring, but one that is clear cut is that a player - or <u>any</u> part of his skate - cannot be in his attacking goal crease until the puck is already there. So, if a goal is scored and the puck was shot from outside the crease, but an offensive player's skate was in the

hat trick

117

crease before the puck got there, the goal will be disallowed (not count). When a player scores three goals in one game, it is known as a **hat trick**. This prompts fans to throw their hats onto the ice. Well, only if it's a player from the home team - who wants to celebrate a guy from the other team scoring three goals?

An **Assist** is given to the player who passed the puck to the player who scored the goal. Or, the player who passed the puck to the player who passed the puck to the player who scored the goal. So, why not the player who passed the puck to the player who passed the puck to the player who passed the puck to the player who scored the goal? Well, so far, the maximum number of players who can be credited for an assist is two. But who knows, maybe in the future when a player is in contract re-negotiations, along with the millions of dollars per year he is claiming he is worth, he may demand he's given credit for assists when he's the "third man out".

Offsides

If there's one thing that can confuse your average hockey fan, it's the **offsides** rule. Actually, the concept itself isn't that difficult to understand, but when watching the game - on television or live - it can be kind-of tough to catch while it's happening. But don't worry, it has nothing to do with your intelligence level, it's because hockey is such an incredibly fast-paced game.

When a team is going from the defensive zone to the neutral zone, the puck must precede the receiver of the pass across the line before he can take possession. For example, let's set-up a little game between "Melrose Place" and "Beverly Hills, 90210". Peter has the puck in his defensive zone, and he sees Michael is open (meaning there are no defensive players around him) in the neutral zone. But Peter cannot pass to him. Why? Because the puck must precede the receiver of the pass, which is Michael, across the blue line.

Remember - the blue line divides the neutral zone from the defensive (and offensive) zone. So, Peter has two options. He can either wait for Michael to come back to the defensive zone, then pass the puck up into the neutral zone and let Michael catch up to it. Or, Peter can bring the puck up into the neutral zone himself, then pass it to Michael.

Now, going from the <u>neutral</u> zone to the <u>offensive</u> zone is a little different. When starting from the neutral zone and going into the offensive/attacking zone, the puck must precede the <u>entire</u> team - not just the receiver of the pass - across the blue line before <u>any player</u> can take possession of the puck. So, Michael now has possession of the puck in the neutral zone. He wants to pass the puck to Amanda, who's waiting in the neutral zone, but another member of his team, say, Jane, is already in the offensive zone. Michael cannot make a pass up into the offensive zone unless his <u>entire</u> team is in the neutral zone.

So, again, he has two choices. He can wait for Jane to come back into the neutral zone, and then pass the puck up into the offensive zone and let Amanda catch up to it. Or, Michael can bring the puck up into the offensive zone himself and then pass it off. Unfortunately, I don't think this game would ever happen. Why? Because I don't see the girls of 90210 playing ice hockey - too many nails would be broken. Except Valerie - Valerie seems like a rough and tough, dropping the gloves kind of girl. Oh, one more thing. The determining factor in offsides is the position of the skates. They must both be over the line ahead of the puck to be considered offsides. So I suppose a player could be at the line, with his stick outstretched ahead, as he attempts to connect with the pass. But as I said, the game is so fast it's pretty difficult to catch the position of the skates as a player is taking off up ice.

You might wonder, why is there an offsides rule? Why keep stopping play unnecessarily? Well, for one, it keeps the number of break-aways and odd-man rushes down. A **break-away** is when a player, in possession of the puck, skates toward the goal with no defensive players between himself and the goaltender. An **odd-man rush** is when a given number of players skate towards their opponents' goal with fewer opposing players between themselves and the goaltender. You'll also hear this referred to as a 3 on 2 situation, or 2 on 1 opportunity. (All right guys, get your minds out of the gutter – again!)

Offside Pass

Within any <u>one</u> zone, there are no restrictions on passing the puck. But a pass that crosses <u>two</u> lines, over a blue and a red line, known as an **offside pass**, is illegal. It's also referred to as a **two line pass**.

Icing the Puck

What in the world could icing mean other than chilling a nice bottle of white wine? Okay, other than the frosting on a cake. Well, in hockey, **icing** is called when a player shoots the puck from his own (defensive) side of the red line, across the

icing the puck

opponents goal line, and is first touched by a defending player other than the goaltender. Now, if either the goaltender or a member of the icing team touches the puck first, it is not considered icing and play continues. But as soon as a defensive player touches the puck, play is stopped and there is a face-off in the icing team's defensive zone. There are two other situations when icing is waived off:

1. the puck passes through any part of the goal crease

2. the goaltender comes out of the crease

You will often see a team intentionally icing the puck just to get it out of their defensive zone when there are a lot of players surrounding the net, in the crease, and the goaltender loses sight of the puck.

• When players (in their offensive zone) position themselves in front of the goaltender in an attempt to block him from seeing where the puck is, it is known as creating a **screen**.

PENALTIES

Obviously in hockey, body contact is allowed. Not only is it allowed, it is encouraged. But believe it or not, there are some rules, and if they're broken, the players are penalized. Actually, let me amend that. If the rules are broken and a player is caught in the act by an official, then he is penalized. And don't you think for one minute that these guys aren't constantly taking cheap shots at each other and hoping to get away with them.

Only the player with the puck is fair game. The opposing team can take the puck away from him by hitting him with a hip or shoulder, called a **body check** - a hip check or a shoulder check - and taking him off the puck. Sometimes a player is hit just seconds after he got rid of the puck, which is legal. But if he clearly no longer has possession of the puck and is checked, a penalty will be given to the player committing an illegal check, known as **interference**.

Another rule is that players must keep their sticks below shoulder level. Players must learn to control their sticks (something guys seem to struggle with practically all their lives), and although accidents happen, a player will be penalized for hitting another player above the shoulder with his stick, accidental or not. This penalty is called **high-sticking**.

<u>Minor Penalties</u>

A minor penalty results in the offender spending the next <u>two minutes</u>, of playing time, while play continues, in the **penalty box**. The penalty box is just off the ice in the neutral zone, opposite the players bench. There is one for each team, and for obvious reasons, they are separated. The offender's team will be **short handed**, and no, it has nothing to do with the size of their hands. It means they will have less players on the ice than the other team because one of their players was a bad boy and was sent to his room - I mean the penalty box.

The other team, consequently, gets a **power play** opportunity, meaning they have a five skater advantage to the other team's four (or three in the case of a double minor when the penalized team has two players in the penalty box). When two opposing players are called for minor penalties at the same time, such as roughing, it is known as **coincidental minors**. The two penalties cancel each other out, and each team still skates with 5 players. Now say one team is on a power play, and one of their players is called for a penalty. That player would go to the penalty box for two minutes, and each team would then have four players on the ice, commonly referred to as **4 on 4**, **4 aside**, or **even strength**. When teams have all their players on the ice, they are skating at **full strength**.

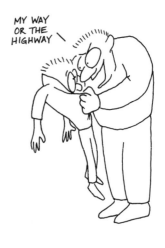

MY WAY OR THE HIGHWAY

power play

During a power play, both teams have a specific group of players on the ice, as designated by the coach. The short-handed team is out there to "kill off" the penalty, so they are referred to as the **penalty-killing unit**. On the other side, the team on the power play has their **power play unit** out on the ice. Both these units are also commonly referred to as **special teams**.

Throughout the penalty, the short handed team has the privilege of being allowed to ice the puck just to get it out of their defensive zone. As soon as the team on the power play scores, the power play is over, even if only a few seconds have elapsed. A penalty is usually called because it interfered with a player's chance to score a goal. Now, if the attacking team retains possession of the puck after the defense commits a penalty, the penalty may not be called immediately. This is usually the case if they are in their offensive zone and in scoring position. The referee will raise his hand to indicate a "foul" has occurred and that there will be a penalty imposed, but not until the <u>defensive</u> team gains possession of the puck. Play is then stopped and the penalty begins. If the team on the power play fails to score, as soon as the penalty is over the player skates out of the penalty box and joins the play without stopping it.

In addition to high-sticking, the following "fouls" result in **minor penalties**, (although there may be some confusion about their definitions.) Therefore, the following should help clarify 1.) the common everyday definition, followed by, 2.) the hockey related definition.

Charging:
1. Using a little plastic card to make purchases. And, coincidentally, this too results in a little penalty called interest.
2. Taking a run at an opposing player, using three or more strides to build up momentum.

Cross Checking:
1. When two people are married, they have cross checking accounts. You deposit money into your account, and withdraw money from his.
2. A block delivered by a player with his stick by placing both hands on the stick with no part of the stick on the ice.

Elbowing
1. When at a mall or crowded bar, this is the only way to get up to the front.
2. Jabbing an opposing player with the elbow, usually at the head or the face.

Holding
1. Showing that special someone affection by putting your arms around them.
2. Grabbing an opposing player's body with the hands. Although I think the "affection" part is missing here.

Hooking
1. The way to catch a good man - get him hooked; cook for him, do his laundry (not too many times), smell irresistible, and wear sexy lingerie.
2. The use of the blade of the stick to trip or interfere with the progress of an opposing player.

Interference
1. When two friends get in an argument, this is how you help make peace between them.

charging

124

2. When a player impedes the progress of an opposing player who is not in possession of the puck.

Roughing
1. As in "roughing it", i.e. camping. You know the scenario – no showers, no make-up, no outlets for your hair dryer....
2. Minor pushing or shoving, which can lead up to full blown fisticuffs.

Slashing
1. What you do to his tires (preferably new ones) if you ever catch him cheating on you.
2. Striking an opposing player's body with the stick.

Tripping
1. What you really want to do to an ex-boyfriend's new "bimbo du jour" when you see them out together. And hopefully she's carrying a glass of red wine.
2. When a player goes flying due to an opposing player using his stick to make him fall.

Bench Penalty

A **bench penalty** is a two minute penalty which is served by any member of the team "off the bench", determined by the coach, if, 1) the goaltender has committed the penalty, or, 2) there are too many players on the ice. And I'm sure that makes the guy who serves the penalty feel good. *You, what's your name, you're not that good, we don't need you out on the ice. Go serve the bench penalty.*

Major Penalties

More serious infractions, such as **fighting**, and committing a minor penalty but drawing blood, result in **major penalties** where the offender must spend the next <u>five</u> <u>minutes</u> in the penalty box. And not only does the other team have that much longer to score a goal while having the extra skater, they can score multiple goals in that time period, the penalty lasting the full five minutes regardless of whether they score or not.

Let me try and explain the difference between "roughing" and "fighting". Roughing is when there's a little shove here, a little push there, no major harm done. Sometimes it's not even reciprocated by the victim of the instigator, which is often smart, because only the shover, not the shovee, will get **the gate** (penalty box) for roughing. Now fighting, that's a different story. A lot of testosterone is flowing here. It starts with a little push here, a little shove there. A few words are exchanged, a little more pushing and shoving, and then the gloves come off. And, sometimes, so does some of their clothing. Sorry, just the jersey, I mean sweater. The officials will usually let this go on for a little while, until one of two things happens: 1) the players hit the ice and a wrestling match ensues, or, 2) a third party, from either team, gets involved.

Here's a sure fire way to tell if it's a full blown fight:

enforcer

Look at the name and number on the back of the jersey. It should look familiar. You might even say to yourself, *hey, he was the guy who was in the last fight, and the fight before that*. Bingo. And the reason that player has been in fight after fight (after fight) is because that is his job. His job is to go out and hit hard, fight hard, and intimidate the other team. He is so important that he has his own special little title - the **enforcer**.

Each team has at least one, although some are more intimidating than others. Now there are also those instances where entire teams become involved. Helmets and gloves and sticks are all over the ice, fists are flying, and officials are trying to break it up without getting a broken nose. It's a huge mess and can take a long time to sort out all the penalties. And if for some reason you missed it (bathroom run?), you can be sure it'll be on the news at ten. I'm telling you, these things are very popular.

Misconduct Penalty

A player is assessed a ten minute **misconduct penalty** for continuing to fight after the officials move in to break it up, or arguing with an official. (They always win, so it's basically pointless for a player to waste his breath.) And only the Captain or Alternate Captain, on the ice at the time (as designated on the sweater by a big "C" or "A") can question the referee.

A misconduct penalty is against the player, not the team, as he is removed from the game for ten minutes, but another player may be substituted into the game for him. A misconduct penalty can also be given out when a 3rd player gets involved in an altercation, for unsportsmanlike conduct, and for major penalties of slashing, high-sticking, and cross checking.

Penalty Shot

When a player has a clear shot at the goal - there are no defenders between himself and the goaltender - but is deliberately interfered with illegally (tripped or hooked from behind), he is awarded a "free shot" called a **penalty shot**. All other players, except the goaltender, clear the ice. The puck is placed at center ice, he can skate in as close to the goal as he likes, and he has one chance to get the puck past the goaltender. The goaltender cannot leave the crease until the player has crossed the blue line. Also, if during the game than the goaltender covers the puck in the crease, a penalty shot is awarded. This is truly one of the most exciting aspects of the game, probably because it doesn't happen often.

THE OFFICIALS

The **referee** - He is in charge of the game. He imposes the penalties, rules on the validity of goals, and supervises the other officials.

The (2) **linesmen** - They watch for offsides and icing and signal the infractions to the referee who stops the play. They conduct all face-offs <u>not</u> at center ice.

(In 1998, the NHL started experimenting using 2 referees and 1 linesman in a number of games in an effort to cut down the number of penalties committed. Is it working? That remains to be seen!)

- The referees and linesmen are the only officials on skates, on the ice, throughout the game. And I would say probably one of the most difficult, yet important, aspects of their job is to get <u>out</u> <u>of</u> <u>the</u> <u>way</u> of the players!

The (2) **goal judges** - They are seated behind each goal and determine if the puck has completely crossed the goal line and entered the net. As soon as the puck crosses the line, he presses a button that turns on a red light above the goal. The goal judge informs the referee that the puck has entered the goal, but it is the referee's job to determine whether the goal scored was, in fact, legal.

For example, if a goal is scored, but an attacking player was standing in the crease before the puck got there, it is the job of the goal judge to turn on the red light. If the referee thinks that the player was in the crease, which the other team will be quick to point out, he will confer with a little man upstairs who will watch a replay of the goal. And all he can tell the referee is if the player was, in fact, in the crease, but none of the is if the player was, in fact, in the crease, but none of the circumstances surrounding him being in there, i.e. if an opposing player pushed him in.

The (2) **penalty box attendants** - They record all information about the penalty, i.e. the player against whom the penalty is called, the violation, and the length of the penalty. They might want to think about wearing protective clothing themselves - some of these players are pretty pissed off when they get in there!

The **game timekeeper** - He records the time of the start and finish of the game and all actual playing time. He indicates the start of the periods to the referee, and brings attention to the end of the period by blowing a whistle or sounding a horn. He also announces when one minute of play remains in each period. I think a requisite of this job is you must have a really deep, sexy voice - you know, the kind that belongs on the radio. I wonder what kind of face goes with that voice!

THE NATIONAL HOCKEY LEAGUE

The National Hockey League (NHL) consists of twenty-seven teams from the United States and Canada. Now I kind-of think it should be called the International Hockey League, considering that it is played in both the US and Canada, and is comprised of players from all over the world. Well, not all over the world, I don't think there are any players from Zimbabwe or Vietnam, but there are a lot from Europe and Russia. Anyway, the League is divided into two conferences, the Western Conference and the Eastern Conference.

Each conference is divided into three divisions; the Central, Northwest, and Pacific divisions in the Western Conference, and the Atlantic, Northeast, and Southeast Divisions in the Eastern Conference.

The 27 teams that make up the National Hockey League are divided as follows:

EASTERN CONFERENCE

Northeast Division

Boston Bruins
Buffalo Sabres
Montreal Canadiens
Toronto Maple Leafs
Ottawa Senators

Atlantic Division

New Jersey Devils
New York Islanders
New York Rangers
Philadelphia Flyers
Pittsburgh Penguins

Southeast Division

Carolina Hurricanes
Florida Panthers
Tampa Bay Lightning
Washington Capitals

WESTERN CONFERENCE

Central Division

Chicago Blackhawks
Detroit Red Wings
Nashville Predators
St. Louis Blues

Pacific Division

Anaheim Mighty Ducks
Dallas Stars
Los Angeles Kings
Phoenix Coyotes
San Jose Sharks

Northwest Division

Calgary Flames
Colorado Avalanche
Edmonton Oilers
Vancouver Canucks

The number of times two teams will play each other in a season depend on the conference and division they are in. Each team plays a team from the other conference two times, once in their own arena, known as a **home game**, and once at the other team's arena, known as an **away game**. Each team plays a team from the same conference/other divisions four times, and the same conference, same division six times. It's just like dating. If you live on the East Coast, you'll be able to go out with guys on the East Coast more often than guys in the Mid-West, or on the West Coast.

For example; the New Jersey Devils (Eastern Conference, Atlantic Division) will play teams from the:

Western Conference - two times, one game at home, one game away.
Eastern Conference, Northeast & Southeast Divisions - four times, two games at home, two games away.
Eastern Conference, Atlantic Division - six times, three games at home, three games away.

Keeping Score

The ultimate goal of every team, in every sport, is to get to the playoffs. And the way to do that is to win games. In hockey, a win is worth two points, a tie one point, and a loss no points. At the end of the season, the top eight teams from <u>each</u> <u>conference</u> advance to the playoffs. If there is a tie for the eighth spot - two teams have the same number of points - the team with more "wins" advances.

THE PLAYOFFS

Question: What is a Stanley Cup? Answer: It is a trophy, (a very, very big silver cup) given to the NHL team that wins the final championship series of the playoffs, known as the **Stanley Cup playoffs**.

There are four rounds in the playoffs, and are each a "best of seven" series, meaning the first team to win four games advances to the next round. When one team wins the first four games in a row, it is called a **sweep**. (A term - a verb - I'm certain many guys are unfamiliar with.) In the first three rounds, the teams only play within their conference. In the first round, the first seeded team will play the eighth seeded team, the second will play the seventh, etc. The second round is cut down to four teams, two games. The third round, down to two teams, one game, is the conference finals. The winner advances to the Stanley Cup championship game, where the two conference champions play for the Stanley Cup. The winners are so proud (and deserve to be) that after being presented the cup, they skate around the rink in celebration with the cup hoisted high above their heads. The cup is eventually engraved with each team member's name right next to the names of last year's winners.

One of the aspects of the playoffs in hockey that makes it so exciting is that the game cannot end in a tie. If at the end of regulation the game ends in a tie, there is a full twenty-minute overtime period. Again, the game ends as soon as someone scores the tie-breaking goal. But, if at the end of twenty-minutes there has been no game-winning goal, there is a full fifteen-minute intermission followed by another twenty-minute overtime period. These games can last for hours. (Just ask the fans of the Washington Capitals about the 4th game of the series versus the Pittsburgh Penguins, on April 24, 1996. It lasted 6 hours and 37 minutes, ending in the 4th overtime!)

And that is the game of hockey.

HOCKEY TALK

"A" - The letter worn on the uniform of the team's alternate captain(s).

Assist - Point awarded to a player(s) for setting up a goal, the last two men to handle the puck prior to the goal scorer.

Attacking/Offensive Zone - The area between the opponents goal and a blue line. (The other team's defensive zone).

Backcheck - An attempt by the forwards, while skating back to their defensive zone, to regain control of the puck.

Bodycheck – Using a hip or shoulder to slow or stop an opponent with the puck.

Breakaway - When a player, in possession of the puck, skates toward the goal with no defensive players between himself and the goaltender.

Breakout Pass - A pass by a team to move the puck out of it's defensive zone.

"C" - The letter worn on the uniform of the team captain.

Carom Pass - A pass that is bounced off/around the boards to a teammate.

Center - The forward who plays between the left wing and right wing, and usually takes the face-offs.

Charging - Taking a run at an opposing player using more than three strides to build up speed. (Minor Penalty)

Crease - The light blue semi-circle in front of the goal.

Cross Checking - A block delivered by a player with both hands on the stick and no part of the stick on the ice. (Minor Penalty)

Defenseman - One of two players whose main responsibility is to help the goaltender protect the goal and prevent the other team from scoring.

Defensive Zone - The area between a team's own goal and blue line. (The other team's attacking/offensive zone).

Drop Pass - When the player with possession of the puck leaves it behind to be picked up by a trailing teammate.

Face-off - When the puck is dropped between two opposing players facing each other to start play.

Forecheck - Applying pressure to the other team in their own (defensive) zone while trying to regain possession of the puck.

Freezing the Puck - Holding the puck against the board with a stick or skates.

Glove Save - When goaltender catches the puck with his glove hand.

Hat Trick - Three goals scored by one player in one game.

Highsticking - Carrying the stick above the shoulders causing an injury to the face or head of an opposing player. (Minor Penalty)

Holding - Grabbing an opposing player's body with the hands. (Minor Penalty)

Hooking - Interfering with an opponent's progress by using the blade of the stick to pull or tug against his body or stick. (Minor Penalty)

Icing the Puck - When a player shoots the puck from his own (defensive) zone across the opponents goal line where it is touched by a defensive player other than the goaltender.

Interference - When a player interferes with the progress of a player who is not in possession of the puck. (Minor Penalty)

Major Penalty - A five minute penalty, usually fighting or any minor penalty that draws blood.

Minor Penalty - A two minute penalty for a "minor" infraction.

Misconduct Penalty - A ten minute penalty against the individual, not the team. Another player may be substituted into the game for him. Called when a player is the first to intervene in an altercation and for major penalties of slashing, high-sticking, and cross checking.

Neutral Zone - Center ice area between the offensive and defensive zones.

Neutral Zone Trap – When a team (on "defense") stays between the blue lines, as their opponents skate towards them, in an effort to cut off the pass and keep them out of their offensive zone.

Odd-man Rush - When a given number of players skate towards their opponents' goal with fewer opposing players between themselves and the goaltender. (Also referred to as a 3 on 2 situation, or 2 on 1 opportunity.)

Offside Pass - Any pass that crosses two lines is illegal, and offside, regardless of the positions of the players.

Offsides - A team is offsides when a player crosses the blue line before the puck.

One-Timer - When a player brings his stick back, and in one motion, he connects with a pass from a teammate and shoots the puck at the goal.

Penalty Box - The area off ice where penalized players serve their time.

Penalty Killing Unit - The specially designed defense used to prevent the other team from scoring while on a power play.

Plus/Minus Rating - Every time a team scores a goal, each of their players on the ice receives a rating of a "plus one", just as each player on the ice receives a rating of a "minus one" when a goal is scored against them.

Poke Check - To dislodge the puck from the puck carrier by stabbing at it with the stick.

Power Play - When a team has more players on the ice because of penalties to the other team.

Power Play Unit – A pre-determined group of players chosen to be on the ice for a power play.

Pull the Goalie - A team down by one goal takes the goaltender off the ice in order to put an extra skater on the ice in an attempt to tie the game. (Usually occurs in the last minute of the game.)

Rebound - A puck that stays in play after the goaltender makes the initial save after a shot on goal but doesn't retain control of the puck.

Roughing - Minor pushing or shoving. (Minor Penalty)

Screen - When players (in their offensive zone) position themselves in front of the opposing goaltender in an attempt to block him from seeing where the puck is.

Short Handed - When a team has less players on the ice than the other team, (and more in the penalty box) due to a penalty on one of it's players.

Shot on Goal - A shot that attempts to score a goal. The puck must be directed to the net with intent to score, and be played by the goaltender. (A shot that misses wide, even if by just inches, does not count as a shot on goal).

Slashing - Striking an opponents body (not stick) with a stick. (Minor Penalty)

Slot - An imaginary triangle defined by the goal and the inside edges of the face-off circles. Considered one of the best places from which to take a shot on goal.

Smothering the Puck - When a goalie or other player falls on the puck and covers it up. It is only legal for the goalie and results in a face-off.

Special Teams - The power play unit and penalty killing unit.

Sweep Check - Using the entire length of the stick, with the lie (heel) of the stick on the ice, in a sweeping motion to get the puck away from an opponent.

Wing - A forward who plays on either the left (left wing) or right (right wing) side of the center.

Wraparound Shot - When a shooter starts from behind the goal and pushes the puck around one goal post in an attempt to get it over the goal line.

Zamboni - The ice resurfacing machine that cleans the surface of the ice. After the first and second period it scrapes snow and ice particles off the surface and puts down a fresh coat of water after the ice has been skated on and cut up.

'Tis the season...

Pool parties... fire works... ice cold lemonade. Can you guess what season it is? I thought you'd say summer. But the season I'm referring to is baseball season. And although sports are played throughout the 4 seasons of the year, rarely can they be categorized by a single season. And that is because between pre-season training camps & exhibition games, the regular season, and the post-season, most sports start in one season and end in another.

Sound a little complicated? Well, it's not really. In fact, you already know that the regular season is the - how can I put this - it's like the entree, the main course, in a four course meal. And you know that the post season is the playoffs, which are a result of a team's performance throughout the regular season. Just think of the post season as the dessert. So let's talk about the pre-season - which I guess could be considered the appetizer and the salad of that four course meal.

The Pre-Season

The pre-season is made up of two parts; **training camp** and **exhibition games**. I would probably say that training camp is somewhere between boot camp and summer camp. I don't think it's hell to make it through, but it's not all fun and games either. There are a few purposes for training camp. One is to get the guys back in "game" shape after a few months off. Lifting weights is good, and some cardiovascular activity is also good, but nothing gets you ready to play the game like playing the game. So this gives the guys a few weeks to practice, as a team, before the real season starts. Another purpose of training camp is to try out recently acquired and prospective players, and see how they fit into the system. There are only so many spots available and everyone needs to prove he deserves to be there. Once the guys are back into shape, (or pretty close to it) and the players settle into their positions, it's time to play the game. But before the regular season begins, the teams have a chance to play a couple practice games, known as exhibition games, against other teams. This primarily helps the team to see where the team's strengths and weaknesses lie, and enables both the coaches and players to make the necessary adjustments.

So, just when do all these games take place? And more importantly, when do they begin and when do they end?

EVENT	DATES
Baseball	
Spring training/exhibition games	Late February to late March
Regular season	Early April to late September
Playoffs (World Series)	Early-mid October
Basketball	
NBA	
Training camp/exhibition games	Early October
Regular season	Early November to mid-March
Playoffs	Late March to early May
College	
Pre-season, training & games	Mid-September to mid-October
Regular season	Mid-October to early March
Playoffs (tournaments)	Mid-March to late March

EVENT	DATES

Football

<u>NFL</u>

Training camp	Mid-July to early August
Exhibition games	Early August to late August
Regular season	Early September to mid-December
Playoffs	Late December to early January
Superbowl	Last Sunday of January

<u>College</u>

Pre-season, training & games	Mid-July to early-September
Regular season	Mid-September to early December
Bowl games	Mid-December to early January

Hockey

Training camp/exhibition games	Early September to early October
Regular season	Early October to mid-March
Stanley Cup Playoffs	Late March to mid-May

QUIZ

Ohhhh.... ugggghhhh... moan and groan.... Come on, it's not that bad. It's just a quiz, and hey, it's not even being graded. Trust me when I say it's for your own good. (Yeah, right, how many times have you heard that one before?!) First of all, it's open book - could it get any easier that that? Yes, you can look back through the book. Or, you could look at the answers of the person next to you. You could even ask the male nearest to you... I'm sure he'll know all the answers, or at least think he does. So get ready... go! (And remember, you are being timed!)

BASEBALL

1. When a player takes a strike, he:

    a. Swings at a bad pitch
    b. Does not swing at a pitch that is in the strike zone
    c. Let's the pitcher hit him

2. A batter walks when:

    a. A wild pitch is thrown
    b. He is too tired to run to 1st base
    c. He receives four balls before he hits the ball
       or strikes out

3. The short stop plays:

    a. Between 2nd and 3rd base
    b. Between the infield and outfield
    c. On an elementary school team

4. The infield fly rule is when:

    a. The batter hits a fly ball within range of the
       infield, he is automatically out
    b. The infielders take a break to make sure their
       fly is up
    c. Only the infield is allowed to catch the ball

5. A bunt is:

    a. A light, fluffy cake
    b. When the batter hits the ball to the pitcher
    c. When the batter lightly taps the ball just a few
       feet from home plate

6. The clean-up hitter:

    a. Bats last
    b. Bats 4th
    c. Sweeps the dirt off home plate

7. A line drive is:

    a. A hard hit ball that travels a long distance with-
       out rising more than a few feet above the ground
    b. When you drive down a one-way street
    c. A ball that rolls down the foul line

8. The tag occurs when:

    a. A player's mom writes his name on the inside
       of his underwear
    b. The catcher runs after the batter to get him out

c. The defensive player touches the runner with the ball before he reaches the base for an out

9. The wild card team is:

   a. The group of guys in the dugout playing cards
   b. The 4th place team in each league that makes it into the playoffs
   c. The team with the most losses

10. A shut-out occurs when:

    a. The pitcher retires 3 batters in a row
    b. The pitcher doesn't allow the opposing team to score any runs
    c. Your wonderfully communicative boyfriend won't tell you what's bothering him when it's so obvious something's wrong

BASKETBALL

11. When a team is in transition, they are:

    a. Going from offense to defense or defense to offense
    b. In between jobs
    c. Making player changes on the court

12. The fast break is when:

    a. You get something by being in the right place at the right time
    b. The offensive team gets the ball downcourt in an attempt to score before the defense sets up
    c. A player brings the ball inbounds and shoots without passing

13. Traveling is:

   a. Living the jet set life
   b. When a player takes consecutive steps without dribbling the ball
   c. Going from offense to defense or defense to offense

14. A player is "in the paint" when:

   a. He gets covered in watercolors
   b. He is in scoring position
   c. He is in the free-throw lane

15. The give and go strategy is when:

   a. The offense turns the ball over and the defense goes to the basket
   b. A guy gives you his best line, and when you tell him to get lost, he goes away
   c. An offensive player gives the ball to a teammate and cuts to the basket before he gets a return pass, enabling him to score

16. The "bench" refers to:

   a. The front row at a game where the celebrities sit
   b. The back-up players who substitute into the game
   c. The area players sit when they've fouled out of the game

17. The "pick and roll" refers to:

   a. A block used on a defensive player to give the ball carrier an open path to the basket
   b. When a defensive player steals the ball and rolls it to a teammate
   c. The name of the arena deli

18. A "one and one" situation occurs when:

    a. A player has to make the first free throw in order
       to get a 2nd free throw
    b. A player believes in monogamy
    c. A team is down to one 20 second and one full time-out

19. Alternating possession occurs when:

    a. You go out with one guy one weekend, and
       another guy the next weekend, then back to the first…
    b. A technical foul is called
    c. A jump ball is called in the college game

20. The 24/35 second rule refers to:

    a. How long it takes most guys to get ready for a date-
       24 seconds, 35 if he puts gel in his hair
    b. The shot clock and how many second a player
       has to shoot the ball
    c. The amount of time one player can have possession
       of the ball before passing it off

FOOTBALL

21. A blitz occurs when:

    a. The quarterback is sacked by more than one lineman
    b. The players get drunk
    c. The secondary gets involved in rushing the quarterback

22. A 4th down conversion is when:

    a. The players change religion
    b. On the 4th down the offense gets enough yardage
       for another 1st down
    c. The two teams switch their offensive and defensive
       teams on the field before the 4th down

23. Another name for the split end is:

   a. Wide receiver
   b. Exterior lineman
   c. Guy with bad hair

24. 2nd and 8 is:

   a. 2nd down, 8 yards to go to reach another 1st down
   b. 2nd half, 8 minutes left in the game
   c. 2nd beer, 8th trip to the bathroom

25. The pass rush is when:

   a. A girl makes it into a sorority
   b. The defense attempts to rush the quarterback
      before he can throw the ball
   c. The quarterback passes the ball, then rushes down
      the sideline

26. The "man in motion" is:

   a. A guy on the prowl
   b. The receiver who gets the ball from the quarterback
      and rushes towards the end zone
   c. The offensive player who runs parallel to the line
      of scrimmage and then back again just before the
      quarterback snaps the ball

27. Special Teams refers to:

   a. Disabled players
   b. Kicking teams
   c. The coach's favorite players

28. Pass interference occurs when:

   a. A player illegally prevents another player
      from catching or intercepting the ball

b. An ex-girlfriend interrupts a romantic evening between you and your boyfriend

c. The quarterback is sacked as he is about to throw the ball

26. A "gain of 5" occurs when:

    a. The offense advances 5 yards
    b. The offense is 5 yards from the end zone
    c. Your jeans are too tight

30. A conference is:

    a. How you and your girlfriends solve a personal problem you're having with your boyfriend
    b. When the offense discusses their plays in the huddle
    c. How schools are grouped together within the NCAA

HOCKEY

31. Icing is not called when:

    a. A white wine is properly chilled
    b. A team is on the power play
    c. The goaltender is out of the net

32. A hat trick occurs when:

    a. A player pulls a bunny out of his helmet
    b. A player scores 3 goals in one game
    c. A player scores a goal short handed, on the power play, and at full strength

33. A body check is when:

    a. Two players from the same team collide
    b. You want to inconspicuously check out the physique of a member of the opposite sex

c. A legal "hit" is made on an opponent using a hip or shoulder

34. A power play is when:

a. Your boss says or does something stupid to remind you who's in charge
b. The players argue with the officials but the officials never listen to them
c. One team plays with more skaters on the ice than than their opponents

35. A line change is when:

a. A group of forwards or defensemen go off the ice as new players go onto the ice.
b. When the coach matches up specific defensive players with the offensive players already on the ice
c. You move to the check-out stand with the fewest people waiting

36. The "crease" refers to:

a. The tiny lines on your forehead you get from too much stress
b. The light blue area around the goaltender
c. The imaginary triangle defined by the goal and the inside edges of the face-off circles.

37. Coincidental minors occur when:

a. A player jumps into a fight to help his teammate
b. 2 opposing players are called for minor penalties at the same time
c. Two people under the age of 21 use the same fake I.D.

38. Offsides occur when:

a. The goalie comes out of the crease

b. You snoop through your roommate's things
c. A player crosses the blue line before the puck

39. The Right Wing/Center/Left Wing refers to:

a. The forwards
b. A 3-piece meal deal
c. The power play unit

40. A screen is:

a. When players (in their offensive zone) position them-selves in front of the goaltender in an attempt to block him from seeing where the puck is
b. When 2 larger players take a smaller player off the puck
c. Useful for keeping insects out of the house

Answers

1.) b	9.) b	17.) a	25.) b	33.) c
2.) c	10.) b	18.) a	26.) c	34.) c
3.) a	11.) a	19.) c	27.) b	35.) a
4.) a	12.) b	20.) b	28.) a	36.) b
5.) c	13.) b	21.) c	29.) a	37.) b
6.) b	14.) c	22.) b	30.) c	38.) c
7.) a	15.) c	23.) a	31.) c	39.) a
8.) c	16.) b	24.) a	32.) b	40.) a

There, that wasn't that bad, was it? And are you not amazed at just how much you now know about sports? Well, I'm impressed. Now go to a game and wow them with all this new knowledge – and have fun!

INDEX